The Young
GREEN
WITCH'S
Guide to
PLANT
MAGIC

· · · · · · · · · · · · · · · ·

RITUALS AND RECIPES
FROM NATURE

· · · · · · · · · · · · · · · ·

ROBIN ROSE BENNETT

Illustrated by RACHEL GRANT

RP | KIDS
PHILADELPHIA

Copyright © 2024 by Robin Rose Bennett
Interior and cover illustrations copyright © 2024 by Rachel Grant
Cover copyright © 2024 by Hachette Book Group, Inc.

Running Press Kids
Hachette Book Group
1290 Avenue of the Americas, New York, NY 10104
www.runningpress.com/rpkids
@runningpresskids

Distributed in the United Kingdom by Little, Brown Book Group UK,
Carmelite House, 50 Victoria Embankment, London, EC4Y 0DZ

First Edition: June 2024

Published by Running Press Kids, an imprint of Hachette Book Group, Inc.
The Running Press Kids name and logo are trademarks of Hachette Book Group, Inc.

The Hachette Speakers Bureau provides a wide range of authors for speaking events. To find out more, go to www.hachettespeakersbureau.com or email HachetteSpeakers@hbgusa.com.

Running Press books may be purchased in bulk for business, educational, or promotional use. For more information, please contact your local bookseller or the Hachette Book Group Special Markets Department at Special.Markets@hbgusa.com.

The publisher is not responsible for websites (or their content) that are not owned by the publisher.

Print book cover and interior design by Frances J. Soo Ping Chow.

Library of Congress Cataloging-in-Publication Data has been applied for.

ISBNs: 978-0-7624-8380-8 (hardcover), 978-0-7624-8381-5 (ebook)

Printed in China

1010

10 9 8 7 6 5 4 3 2 1

Contents

. . . .

Letter to the Reader

Dear Reader:

What is a green witch anyway?

Green witches don't like to be boxed in by anyone else's definition of who we are, but there are a few key points upon which we can agree.

Green witches love the Earth and know the Earth loves us. We know that plants have secrets to share and gifts to give, so we learn all we can about nature, especially herbs, flowers, and trees. We make a choice to respect and connect with the abundance and strength of the Earth, which helps *us* grow stronger and more confident. Plants guide us to love ourselves, inside and out, and to take care of our minds and bodies. We like to help plants grow, but when we pay close attention to them, we realize *they* "grow" *us*.

We strive to embrace and accept everything about ourselves, even the stuff that we may judge negatively, like feeling anxious, scared, or not good enough. We're all made of many parts. Green witches encourage each other to remember we are magical, strong, beautiful, unique, open-minded, open-hearted, and grounded. We are also sparkling, cosmic beings made of stardust!

A scientific study published in 2017 on Space.com confirmed "Humans have about 97 percent of the same kind of atoms as our galaxy. A new study has mapped the elements found in the human body, the building blocks of life, and they are the same as those found in the hundreds of thousands of stars in our Milky Way."

I invite you to explore this green witch way of looking at the world because of how much it's helped me and so many others I've taught. It started when I was eighteen and looking for help with some health problems I'd suffered from since I was a little kid. I learned that there were natural ways for me to become healthier, but what I found as I went on went deeper. The world was becoming much larger than just my family and friends, and I was discovering that magic was everywhere.

That feeling has only grown. I am still called "The Green Witch of New York" because I lived in downtown New York City for the first ten years I was an herbalist. My great-grandma, Esther, was also a city green witch. She lived in Brooklyn, New York, a long, long time ago. I promise you that once you open your eyes and heart to the green healers, you will become aware that you are part of a living, loving community anywhere you go on planet Earth.

As you learn to create food, medicine, art, spells, and rituals in partnership with the natural world of which you are an integral part, you'll discover that real life is far more magical than you might think! That's why I want to help you learn to look into nature as if you're looking into a mirror; let it reflect how beautiful, strong, and gifted you truly are. Each one of us has something totally unique to offer this world.

Being outside in nature helps us feel joyful as we connect with the incredible energy of the plants around us. The plants "know" who they are and are secure in the fact that they are exactly where they belong. When we eat and drink them, or meditate, make art, or do rituals with them, they help us know who *we* are, and where *we* belong. I'm excited for you to experience this for yourself as you get to know the plants featured in this book.

Each plant chapter includes that plant's most special magic, a poem in which the plant talks to you directly, identification and gathering tips, and a variety of hands-on activities, from cooking and making teas to fun, witchy crafts that will help you explore the plant's magic and herbal medicine. Of course, suggestions of how, when, and why to work with the plant magically in spells and rituals will be included, too.

Green witches often start their journey by choosing one plant at a time to become best friends with. That plant becomes your first "plant ally," offering you healing and teachings that will help you grow. Your plant ally can help you feel safe in your body, seen for who you are, and loved and supported to become ever more joyful. We'll explore ways to help you "listen" to the plants, connect more deeply with the Earth as the living goddess that she is, trust your intuition, and tune into your own inner wisdom for 24/7 guidance. How do I know? Because I've watched it happen over and over again for every single person who decided to dare to listen to a plant.

This good green magic connects us with each other, too, as a loose-knit community, in which everyone is allowed and encouraged to be who they truly are. I am writing this book to encourage young green witches, or as I like to say, green witchlets, to become who you came here to be: yourself!

There is only one *you*, and you matter! A lot!

And remember: no matter how much we learn, we'll never know everything. And that's okay because it's much more fun to keep an open mind, and keep learning and discovering new things about ourselves and the world around us.

The plants are waiting for us.

Green blessings,
Robin Rose Bennett

~*~

Green Witch, Herbalist

Nature
Is Alive

. . . .

EVERYTHING IS ALIVE. *EVERYTHING*. NOT ONLY THE ANIMALS, but the plants, the soil, the water (the oldest of the elements), and even the stones. Consider, for example, quartz crystals, which are a common part of cell phones, television receivers, watches, and clocks.

They pulse with an inner life force that we can apply for our own uses. Whether powering our phones and laptops, or being cut and shaped to be worn as magical jewelry, the crystals respond. They are alive.

One of the main reasons quartz crystal is used in so many electronic devices is because it is piezoelectric, meaning it generates an electric charge when pressure is exerted upon it.

The understanding that everything in nature is truly alive and is a vital part of the web of life is a completely natural idea to Indigenous people. And to green witches! Within this worldview is the knowledge that we live in an intimate relationship with the land and we respect the interconnected web of life and the spiritual force that animates everything in existence.

1

In western cultures, though the majority of people may not necessarily feel a deep connection with the land on which they live, or the city block upon which their apartment building sits, when we open our senses to our kinship with the living world, we deepen our sense of respect for, and belonging to, the living land. Green witches enjoy learning all we can about the land we live on, such as how old the land is and what watershed we belong to. Where does the water in your area collect? Where does it drain out to? It is also respectful to learn the Indigenous history of the land where you live. Do you know who lived there originally? Are they still present? The original inhabitants of the wooded forest land where I live are the Lenape, and they are still here. Seeking out elders who live nearby, Indigenous and otherwise, can be a great opportunity to learn new things about where you live, including stories you may not be able to find in books. I learned that the forest behind my home was once the bottom of the ocean.

When I first started exploring herbal medicine, I thought of herbs as merely ground-up powders in little packets at the store that might make my health problem go away. However, coming to herbs from the perspective of a green witch, and connecting with plants as *beings*, led me to slowly but surely feel like I belonged in the world in a way that I never really had before. I found myself part of a living, loving community of kinship that included the more-than-human world.

When we understand that plants are living beings with feelings and awareness, we recognize that the plants are sharing their gifts with us. It is in their nature to do so. We are in this world together. Think about it: every single moment of your life you inhale what the plants exhale—oxygen—and they inhale what you exhale—carbon dioxide. That is an intimate friendship, a bond for life.

The Magic of Plants

The plants in this book offer us physical, spiritual, mental, and emotional healing on the deepest levels of our beings. Think of how long it can take to really get to know a person. Maybe you sit behind someone in homeroom on the first day of school and overhear something they say that makes you laugh. Later, you might see them at their locker between classes and make plans to have lunch together. Over lunch you talk and discover things about each other that make you want to know them even better.

It is the same with any plant. At first, maybe you're drawn to them because you like how they look—ooh, rose is so beautiful. Or how they smell—mmm, lavender smells good. Maybe you drink a cup of mint tea and like how it tastes. That's just the surface, though. There's so much more to learn! Just as you get to know different sides of a person in different situations, the same happens with plants. When you take time to be observant, you might see, for example, that dandelion flowers open wide in the sunshine and close tight in the rain. And that might get you wondering if dandelions could help *you* open to light, open to more joy and happiness. And you know what? They can!

Plants are wise beings. They live in reciprocal relationships with the birds and animals around them, including us.

A reciprocal relationship is one in which everyone is both giving and receiving from one another. Reciprocal blessings are when what is being exchanged is valuable and makes life better than it would be otherwise. True friendship is a reciprocal blessing.

Imagine that a robin (the bird, not me) nibbles blueberries from a bush, then flies off, saying, "Thank you, blueberry!" Later, the robin plants the seeds by pooping them out somewhere else, giving all of us more blueberry bushes, which leads to more yummy blueberries, and the blueberry bush can say, "Thank you, robin, for planting my children!"

In another example, plants absorb the minerals they need from the soil in which they live. When perennial plants go back down into the earth in the winter to await rebirth in the spring, they transmit those minerals back into the soil, keeping it fertile so they and other plants can grow healthy and strong there.

A perennial plant is one that dies down each winter and comes back each spring. All of the plants presented in this book are perennials, with different life spans, except for oatstraw (*Avena sativa*), which is an annual plant. Like any annual, after an oat plant produces seeds, ensuring the next generation of oat plants, the mother plant dies. And in dying, the plant's body breaks down (decomposes) and nourishes the soil. When the Earth is well-fed, she grows more plants to feed everyone.

When we look at nature closely, we see that we are offering healing and nourishment to one another all the time. Everything on Earth is woven together in a beautiful web of interconnection. A web of love. We belong to one another.

Green witches talk to plants, but we also strive to listen to them because they have secrets to share and wisdom we need to know. For instance, roses can teach us how to keep our hearts open and be kind, even when we have to say, "No." They teach us this through their sweet, welcoming fragrance and sharp, piercing thorns. You will learn to hear the "voice" of nature, too, if you don't already, and you'll receive messages that are meant just for you, messages that will guide and support you in your practice.

Plants know who they are and love themselves for who they are. I never met a willow tree that wished it were a cinnamon tree. (Did you know cinnamon is a tree?) Or a dandelion that wished it were a rose. Oh no. Dandelions are quite pleased with their own weedy, rougher beauty. And they are tough, too. Dandelions are resilient. They don't give up! We have a lot to learn about self-acceptance from plants. And loving and accepting yourself is the most important teaching of all. It leads to inner peace, which leads to peace in our families and in the world.

Approach plants and trees with an open mind. Gratitude will come easily as you begin to experience all the amazing things they can do, and as you begin to feel their love for you. Respect, too, comes naturally when you stop and pay attention. It all starts with *slowing down* to spend time with them.

These are just some of the reasons green witches thank the herbs, trees, and flowers when we gather any of their parts for food and medicine. It is also simply polite. Plants have feelings, too. They respond well to consideration, gratitude, appreciation, and tender loving care, just like anyone else.

Healing plants are everywhere—whether you live in the country, the suburbs, or even the city. Plants are our elders. They arose on Earth long before us and, in that sense, we are all their children. And though they don't speak in words, we can learn their languages of color, texture, taste, temperature, location, and more.

Wildcrafting

"Wildcrafting" is the herbal term used to describe gathering wild plants. A person who gathers wild plants for any purpose is called a "wildcrafter," while "forager" is the term used for someone gathering wild plants to eat. Green witch herbalists love to do both! It is vital that you know you are picking the correct plant. And as a forager and wildcrafter who cares deeply about the health of the Earth, it is also essential to know how much of that plant is sustainable to gather. We learn this one plant at a time.

If you are looking to gather from someone else's land or garden, of course don't just ask the plant. Ask the person whose land it is on for permission before picking any flowers or leaves! Know the rules of local parks, as well. Always make sure pesticides have not been sprayed before you gather plants to use for food or medicine. I like to suggest that if you discover pesticide use somewhere, speak up for using natural, organic, health-promoting approaches to taking care of private or public lands. You might be surprised how you can effect change in your local community. Your love for the plants can be a powerful force in helping change things for the better.

To gather plants, you will first need to learn to identify them correctly. This may be done with the help of a knowledgeable adult, or an herbalist or naturalist in your area. You can also use a field guide to aid you.

Learning to identify the plants in this book and also growing some plants in your garden or indoors will help you feel grounded and more confident. These are skills you will use your whole life. You will get to know the land where you live and to feel more at home in it. You always need to learn about a plant in relation to its environment. How abundant is it? Does it grow best in the sun or the shade? In dry soil or moist? Is the land clean of pesticides or other pollutants? Is there a factory or industrial farm just upstream? We want to work with the land in ways that do no harm and that help us take care of it. A general guideline for wildcrafting is to only gather plants that are abundant, and take no more than 10 to 15 percent of the plant you are harvesting from one area.

Green witches focus on working with the most common weeds for our magic and medicine. You might be thinking: *weeds*?! Aren't they the plants we want to get rid of? What's in a name? I've noticed people seem to like weeds a whole lot better when we call them wildflowers! Seriously, though, they are the same plants. The reason green witch herbalists favor using wild plants, a.k.a. "weeds," is because they are hearty, abundant, and resilient—ask any gardener who tries to get rid of them! You've probably heard the expression "you are what you eat." Well, we take these "weedy" qualities into ourselves when we ingest these wild plants as food, or drink them as medicinal teas. It's empowering to know which wild plants contain the most amazing properties, the chlorophyll, vitamins, minerals, and more that strengthen us, or soothe pain, among the many ways they can help us heal ourselves.

Of course you can purchase dried herbs, and sometimes fresh ones from herb shops, at farmers' markets, and by mail order. But whenever possible, green witches want to learn how, when, and where to gather our own plants, using our physical senses of sight, touch, smell, and taste. Developing this skill, however, takes patience. Learning to slow down and observe nature more closely also helps you tune in and trust your intuition. This helps us be true to ourselves and make choices that feel good to us, and to the Earth.

Green Witch Plant Rituals

· ·

THESE SIMPLE RITUALS WILL HELP YOU GET TO KNOW THE plants you are working and playing with better, while, in turn, allowing each plant to get to know *you* better. They will also help you develop and deepen your intuition. I think you'll enjoy practicing these rituals again and again while you are getting to know each of the plants in this book.

HARVESTING RITUAL—
ASKING FOR PERMISSION
AND GIVING THANKS

WHETHER SILENTLY OR ALOUD, GREEN WITCHES ALWAYS ASK permission and give thanks before harvesting plants, especially when gathering them from the wild.

Because many of us did not grow up being taught that plants are *beings* deserving of respect, this ritual of asking a plant for permission to harvest, and waiting for the answer before proceeding, is a good practice for green witches; it helps us tune into the plants more fully, both with our physical senses and our inner senses.

Imagine for a moment that you are about to pick some basil leaves from your herb garden or a pot on your windowsill. Silently or aloud, whatever feels most comfortable to you, communicate your intention to your basil plant: "I'd like to harvest some of your leaves for pesto. May I?" Your plants are almost always happy for you to harvest and use them, but it's still polite to ask! Of course, if you get a sense *not* to harvest, look more closely. Maybe the plants need to be tended to, and perhaps it's time to take care of them instead of taking them for yourself.

Here are a few ideas to help you get started listening to plants. Picture "yes" as a green light and "no" as a red light. Close your eyes and see which light is shining stronger. You may feel a warmth in your heart when a plant wants you to work together, whereas another young green witch might literally hear "yes" or "no," as if the plant is speaking inside their mind. Others may find goose bumps, which I call "truth bumps," raising on their arms. You'll find your own ways of understanding how the plants communicate with you and how your inner voice is guiding you as you practice and gain your own experiences.

Now, assuming a plant gives you the go-ahead, I encourage you to quietly say or think "thank you" with each leaf you gently pick.

GIVE-AWAY RITUAL–
GROWING GRATITUDE

THIS RITUAL INVOLVES PLACING SOMETHING NATURAL AT THE base of a plant or tree as an offering of gratitude for the gift the plant is about to share with you.

Any variety of natural substances can be used for your give-away, so start with something that will return easily to the Earth to be broken down by the bacteria in the soil. You can offer fresh water when the soil is dry, or a beautiful leaf or flower that you find, or perhaps a stone or crystal from your personal collection. Even a piece of your own hair will do in a pinch! Whatever you choose, it's important that you give away something that matters to you and/or that you think is beautiful, or that the plant may need.

The practice of giving thanks before you actually receive something you desire is an important component in magical spells and rituals, too.

CRAFTING A
GIVE-AWAY/GRATITUDE BUNDLE

YOU'LL NEED:

3 or more dried herbs that you like, for example:
lavender, roses, and peppermint or spearmint

Small fabric bag

DIRECTIONS:

- Mix the herbs together in whatever proportions you like.
- When you are pleased with the blend you've created, put the herbs into a small fabric bag.
- You can keep it simple or decorate the bag, sewing or gluing favorite shells or charms onto it, or drawing or painting on it.

The essence of this ritual is: you are giving something to the plant in return for what you are receiving, whether what you are asking for is a feeling of remembered connection, physical healing, spiritual knowledge, magical results, leaves for tea, flowers or vines for crafting a wreath, sweet fruits to eat, or in the case of harvesting roots, the plant's life. This ritual also reminds us that whatever we choose to give, we have received it from the Earth in the first place.

CONNECTION RITUAL

ONE OF THE MOST DIRECT WAYS TO OPEN A CHANNEL OF communication with any plant is through a basic ritual of connection. Use this ritual practice to get to know a plant in your backyard, on your street, or in the woods—including plants whose names you don't know, but that you feel drawn to or called by. You can do this on your own or together with one or more friends who are also budding green witches.

1. Sit comfortably, facing the plant. (If you are doing this exercise with a tree, you may want to stand with your back to the tree trunk. Choose whatever position feels right for you.)

2. Take an easy, deep breath in, and exhale with a sigh, or with any sound you feel like making. Do this a few times, until you feel yourself more relaxed. Tune in to any places in your body that may feel tense, and each time you exhale, invite these tense places to soften. This will relax your mind, too.

3. Silently introduce yourself and imagine the plant looking at you, just like you are looking at them. You might want to invite them to really *see* you, just as you are asking to be allowed to really *see* the plant, asking them to reveal their magic to you.

4. Imagine that the next breath you inhale is coming to you directly from the plant. Receive it as a gift, right in the center of your chest, in your energetic heart center.

5. When you exhale, imagine that you are giving your breath, from your heart, as a gift to the plant, who is opening to receive it from you, with gratitude.

When we slow down and breathe together, living being to living being, we meet the plants where they are. Continue this practice of paying attention to the breath flowing easily back and forth between you and the plant. Imagine it creating the infinity symbol, a figure 8, connecting you from the center of your heart to the center of the plant. Do this for as long as you like, but try to stay with it for at least 5 minutes.

When you are finished, notice how you feel. If you're not sure you felt anything, that's okay. It's like learning a new musical instrument or a sport. You get more confident the more you practice, and the more time you give it.

If you are with others, you can compare notes, feelings, messages, and any other impressions after you sit quietly for a bit.

Your Green Witch Journal

You'll want to have a special book where you can write down your experiences. This journal is a space for your feelings, questions, and discoveries, so you can review and learn from them. It's helpful to record your flops (we all have them) and successes (we all have these, too) as you explore rituals and recipes, spells and meditations, your plant discoveries, and just as importantly, your discoveries about yourself.

Did you know that your brain works differently when you write by hand than when you type? It's true! Writing by hand generates activity in the part of your brain that helps you to have a stronger understanding of the subject you are exploring.

There are a few names for this kind of book. One name is "grimoire"—pronounced grim-war (war rhymes with car). Another popular term is "Book of Shadows." Whatever you decide to call it, you'll want to record all your herbal and magical explorations. You can write and draw in it, press plants between its pages, note impressions from meditations and rituals, record results of spells, and copy or create new recipes. Add anything else you discover about the world around you, and/or about yourself that is connected to this journey into the world of nature that you're now traveling along, guided by the magic of the plants.

I like to write in mine with a purple pen and draw and doodle with colored pencils, and I paste things in there, too. Yours can be a safe place to freely explore all the things you try out. Some years I've used beautiful leather-bound books filled with handmade paper, and yet I often like to use a simple notebook with unlined, recycled paper that has heavy covers I can decorate with pictures from nature calendars. I also put the start and end date of each of my green witch journals on the front and back pages. I have quite a collection at this point!

Please feel free to use any kind of journal you like, lined or unlined, large or small. Plain or fancy, decorated or unadorned. *You* will make it a *magic book* with what you put inside!

Rose

(*ROSA* SPECIES)
SELF-LOVE AND CLAIM-YOUR-SPACE MAGIC

• •

Also known as: dog rose, sweet briar, field rose
Rose says: "Love yourself, just the way you are."

Meet Rose

See my blossoms open wide,
I don't have a thing to hide.
In the fall my hips turn red,
They taste tangy, that's what's said.
When you drink me in your tea
I help to set your loving free.
Yet my thorns are present, too,
I am watching out for you.
I truly care how you feel
And I love to help you heal.

Herbal Healing

Roses are a beloved, highly valued herbal medicine all around the world. They are part of an enormous family of plants that includes well-known fruits and nuts such as raspberries and blackberries, peaches and strawberries, and almonds and apples, all of which promote good health.

Roses aid circulation of the blood through our veins and arteries and are a tonic for the heart. They are anti-infective and anti-inflammatory, supporting our immune systems. Rose also strengthens the kidneys and cools down the liver, which helps us to have healthy digestion and balance our hormones. They can help us heal from burns and bug bites, and they're rightfully famous for helping our skin!

And though I would never make light of all the profound physical benefits rose has to offer us, I must admit that I most frequently use and suggest roses for uplifting our spirits, delighting our senses, and for emotional soothing. And for love magic and rituals.

Rose has been the prized national flower of Iran for centuries, dating back to when Iran was known as Persia. In the Atlas Mountains of Morocco, one of the most popular public celebrations is the annual rose festival. Damask roses scent the air in the Valley of Roses, and a young girl is crowned the Rose Queen for the three-day festival.

Working with Rose

Rose, especially *wild* rose, is the flower of love. There are many aspects to a rose, from her soft, inviting blossoms to those sharp, forbidding thorns! In the same way, there are many aspects to love—love for self, love for others, love for life—and rose helps us feel them all!

Many different species of roses can be used in herbal medicine and magic, from the wildly weedy *Rosa multiflora* with small white flowers to *Rosa rugosa*, also known as beach rose. Rugosa means "wrinkled" and refers to the wrinkled leaves.

Both of these common species are native to China, Japan, Siberia, and other far eastern lands, though they have naturalized far and wide. Another lovely, abundant, wild rose with pink blossoms is *Rosa canina*, the dog rose, native to Europe, northwest Africa, and western Asia. There are native North American roses, too, such as the lovely and prolific *Rosa virginiana* and *Rosa carolina*, which both have wide-open pink blossoms.

Native plants are plants that are believed to have always grown in a particular area. Naturalized plants are ones that have fully integrated into a new home and reproduced there. Sometimes, naturalized plants can take over habitats and crowd out native species. These are labeled invasive. However, I prefer the term pervasive, which simply means they are *very* abundant. Invasive sounds sinister, as if the plants have an evil intention, which they don't. Many, though not all, pervasive plants bring us food and medicine, as well as provide healing to land, air, and water.

I suggest you don't use roses that have been so highly bred they have no fragrance, as it is an essential part of this plant's healing properties.

Rose is a plant that invites you to come home to yourself in a very special way, teaching you through her magic and medicine how to open to receive what nourishes and feels good inside you, and how to say "no" to that which is hurtful, or not right for you.

Rose Hips

Ovary

Petiole

Stipules

Identifying Rose

Let's focus on wild roses. What the various wild rose bushes have in common is that their flowers are pink or white, and the petals are symmetrically sized and shaped. These roses have five petals and five sepals, with numerous stamens, and they smell distinctly sweet.

Scientific estimates suggest there may be more than thirty thousand varieties of roses in the world! Cultivated roses are typically bred to have more petals and a range of different colors. Some have that distinctive rose fragrance, and others do not.

Wild roses have paired, oval-shaped leaves consisting of either four or eight leaflets with one leaflet on the end. These leaves are serrated (toothed).

Another thing that can help you identify roses is that they often have stipules. Stipules are small, leaf-like outgrowths on the leaf stalk.

The leaf stalk, called a "petiole" in botany, is the little stem that attaches the leaf to the main stem. Behind each flower, right in the center, is the part of the blossom called the ovary, and here is where the fruit of the rose grows. The ovary will begin to grow rounder, causing the flower petals to open wider until they eventually fall off. Then the rose hip will continue to ripen, turning from green to red. The rose "hips" are seedy fruits that ripen to a deep red color after the first frost of the season, and that frost makes them taste sweeter, too. This fruit is edible and medicinal!

We can't talk about identifying roses without mentioning their infamous thorns! Botanically, rose thorns are actually called "prickles" because they grow from the surface tissue of the plant, but whatever we call them, they are pointy and sharp, and they serve to protect the rose!

Roses are found in all kinds of soil, from rich garden loam to compacted wastelands, and though they prefer sun, they will grow in shade, too. Roses are hardy plants!

Gathering Roses

Depending on where you live, you can gather the flowers beginning in late spring and continuing all summer long. You can harvest roses whenever they are in bloom! It's best to gather roses when they have partially or fully opened. You want to remove them from the stalk when they're fresh and not yet wilted by the sun, but after the dew has evaporated off the petals. Any time in the late morning or early to midafternoon is usually good. Reach behind a flower, pinch it off the stalk, then gently place the whole blossom in your bag or gathering basket.

There are so many fun things you can do with roses, and how much to gather will depend on how many roses you have access to, in the wild or in your garden. Be aware that whenever you harvest a rose blossom, one less rose hip will be available for the wildlife to eat and/or for you to gather in the autumn.

It is traditional to harvest the hips after a frost has had a chance to concentrate the vitamins C and E they contain, and to soften their outer skin. These days, with the climate shifting so radically, another option is to pick your rose hips when they are ripe and red in the autumn and put them into the freezer for twenty-four hours to mimic the first frost before removing them.

Rose hips left on the bushes will be enjoyed by birds all winter and will help nourish animals such as squirrels, bears, and deer in the early spring when wild food tends to be scarce. However, when it comes to wild roses like *Rosa multiflora*, there is often more than enough for all of us! You can pick the individual, large *Rosa rugosa* hips off the branches. However, if you're gathering the very small hips of *Rosa multiflora*, you can gather whole clusters of them at once, rather than one at a time. The thin twigs that hold them will snap fairly easily.

Lay the blossoms out on wicker trays, screens, or even paper towels. Dry them away from direct sunlight, touching each other as little as possible. When they are thoroughly dry, they should no longer feel supple. Place the dried roses in a clean, dry paper bag. Label your bag with the common and botanical names (for practice) and the month, year, and place they were growing.

TIP: If you label the bag near the bottom, as you use up your roses, you will still be able to read what's inside.

Creativity in the Kitchen

Roses are highly valued in cuisines around the world, from Italy to Iran, Afghanistan to India, throughout the Middle East, the Balkans, and in parts of China, Japan, and Africa, but their use in the kitchen isn't only limited to food. Rose, often called the "Queen of Flowers," is prized for her beauty and medicinal benefits, too. From tinctures to balms and everything in between, here are some suggestions for how to bring rose into your own kitchen!

ROSE-INFUSED VINEGAR

||||||||||||||||||||||||||||||||||||||||||||||||||||||||||||||||||||

This simple recipe is excellent for use on sunburns or to soothe bug bites. It works topically to ease swelling and prevent infection. Keep this handy for soothing your skin when it's red or irritated. Do not use vinegar directly on swollen eyelids. (Witch hazel from the pharmacy is perfect for that, though.) Rose vinegar is also lovely when added to a bath! Pour about ½–1 cup in your bathtub to soften and nourish your skin. It is also edible and makes a great salad dressing!

continued

INGREDIENTS:

3½ cups *fresh roses

1 quart apple cider vinegar

*or 2 cups dry, if fresh petals are unavailable

DIRECTIONS:

- Fill a 1-quart glass jar with fresh roses, torn or cut into pieces.
- Cover with apple cider vinegar and cap with a lid. (A plastic lid is best, as it prevents rust, but if you don't have a plastic lid, line your metal lid with a piece of unbleached parchment paper or plastic wrap.)
- Leave the jar out on the counter for 2–4 weeks.
- When it's ready, pour off the liquid into a container with a spout. Squeeze the roses to get the last of the good medicine.
- Compost the roses outside.

ROSE VINEGAR—QUICK METHOD

Slow infusing brings out the *best* in the rose vinegar, but sometimes you just can't wait. Put your roses and vinegar (same amounts as above) into a 1-quart saucepan. Bring the mixture to just below boiling, then turn off the heat. Let the rose vinegar sit covered for 30–60 minutes. Then pour off the rose vinegar into a bottle, let it cool, squeeze out the roses, and you can use it immediately. Try making it both ways so you can compare them.

ROSE BLOSSOM HONEY

‖‖

My all-time favorite rose blossom preparation is infused rose honey. It is so easy to make, and it tastes *delicious*! The sweetness of honey brings out rose's unique fragrance to perfection!

INGREDIENTS:

1 cup *fresh roses (any fragrant, unsprayed variety)
1 pint local wildflower or clover honey
*or ¼–½ cup dry, if fresh petals are unavailable

DIRECTIONS:

- Cut or tear the fresh rose blossoms finely. (If using dry roses, crumble the blossoms with your hands.)
- Put them into a 1-pint glass jar, loosely packed, until it is almost full.
- Slowly cover them with honey. Use a chopstick, stick, or other thin tool to poke around through the flowers and make sure all the petals are fully saturated with the honey. Add more honey as needed to fill the jar all the way to the top.
- Set your jar atop a plate, as the honey may ooze out and is likely to make a sticky mess while it is infusing.
- Label the lid of your jar with the botanical name of the roses, if you know it.

continued

- If you don't, write *Rosa spp.*, which means "some species of rose." Write the date you made it, and any pertinent information (see sample label below). I suggest putting the label on the lid because if the honey overflows, it can blur or erase what you wrote. Or you can label both the lid and the jar. Your label might look something like this:

ROSA SPP.
day / month / year

- This preparation will get better and better for as long as it sits steeping, but you can start to sneak tastes within hours!
- When it's ready, you can use the honey with the cut-up petals still in it. Spread it on toast or pancakes, or stir it into tea.

ROSE BLOSSOM HONEY FACIAL MASK

You can also put the rose blossom honey on your face!

Tie back your hair, if needed, and either dip your clean fingers into the honey, or if you prefer, spoon out a bit with a tablespoon. Using light strokes, apply it all over your face except on your eyelids.

Use upward sweeps as you apply a layer of infused rose honey onto your cheeks and chin and then smooth it across your brow. You can also sweep it up your neck if you like. Wait 5–15 minutes before rinsing this off with warm water, using a washcloth to make sure all the honey is removed. Your skin will be glowing and you will feel amazing!

ROSE BLOSSOM TEA

A cup of rose tea is almost guaranteed to put a smile on your face and in your heart. If you have been sunburnt, or you feel sad or blah, rose tea will soothe and brighten your mood. You can drink it sweetened with your rose blossom honey for added delight.

INGREDIENTS:

1 teaspoon dried roses (pink or red)

1 cup boiling water

DIRECTIONS:

- Put the dried roses in your mug, or sit them inside a tea strainer in the mug.
- Pour the boiling water over the roses to fill the mug, and steep them for 10–15 minutes.

ICED ROSE BLOSSOM TEA

If you want to make an iced version for a refreshing drink on a hot day, here's a recipe to make a pitcher.

Put ¾ cup of dried roses in a ½-gallon jar or pot. Cover with 2 cups of boiled water. Let steep for 30 minutes. Strain out the roses. Pour the tea into a pitcher and add cold water and ice to fill the jar. You can sit a metal spoon in there to conduct some of the heat if you're at all concerned about breakage. Refrigerate if needed. Enjoy!

ROSE HIP INFUSION

This tart, tangy, tasty infusion is rich in vitamin C and supports you in staying strong and healthy or in getting over a cold or flu if you've gotten sick. Rose hips will give you stamina, too.

INGREDIENTS:

1½ cups dried rose hips

1 quart boiling water

DIRECTIONS:

- Put the rose hips into a 1-quart glass jar.
- Pour the boiling water over the hips.
- Cap the jar tightly and let it sit out overnight.
- Pour off the infusion, then compost your rose hips.
- Heat and enjoy by the mugful, sweetened or not.

Rose in Magic and Ritual

Rose is simply the best plant of all for helping you open yourself to both giving and receiving love. Rose wants you to accept yourself fully. She teaches you how to say "yes" to self-care and kindness and "no" to things that aren't healthy for you, or are unkind.

She also helps you extend the same kindness to others. Rose helps you listen to other people's points of view. If you are in a fight with your friend or someone else you love dearly, and the two of you haven't been able to find a way to forgive or even understand each other, have a cup of rose tea together. I've seen this magic at work. It's as if rose cleans out a stuffed-up place in your ears that won't let you hear the other person, and suddenly you can, and your heart opens up! And that always feels good.

Rose's thorns are powerfully symbolic of "claiming your space." They remind you that your body belongs to you! You can call on those thorns psychically, in your imagination, and ask them to help you grow strong in yourself. Her flowers bring in the beauty of life. When we drink rose, we are drinking the beauty of the Earth herself.

A ROSE RITUAL

Creating a Doorway of Initiation—
Crossing the Threshold of Love

THIS CAN BE DONE ALONE, AS ALMOST ANY RITUAL IN THIS book can, but it is probably more fun and powerful to do it with a small circle of young green witches, or even two of you.

Pick an outdoor spot in a meadow or a backyard where you can be safe, yet have privacy. You'll need rose hip infusion, rose blossom honey, and about 6–8 cups of dried roses. You're also likely to want to have chocolate for the celebration at the end of the ritual. Chocolate and roses go very well together!

Spread the roses in a line about 3 feet long to create a magical threshold. Ideally, spread the roses between two trees, but you can be creative; use what's available to you. Perhaps a special stone on each end of the rose threshold marks the doorway.

Sit in a semicircle on one side of the threshold, facing the roses, and envision a protective circle of love forming all the way around you and the magical doorway you have created. Share a cup of rose hip infusion, and sit quietly for a few minutes. Focus on your breathing to move into a gentle meditation. In your meditation, ask rose to help you say "yes" to yourself. Make a promise to practice loving and accepting yourself no matter what, even if you make a mistake, or say the wrong thing, or people tell you you're too loud, or too shy, or you feel silly, or anything else! You can also ask rose to help you grow some thorns of your own if you feel like you are too "nice" all the time. After a few minutes, one of you will walk out of the semicircle and circle around to the other side of your magical doorway. When you are on one side of the threshold, and your friends are on the other, they will witness you "crossing" and will be there waiting to welcome you once you've crossed over to a new place of being kind to yourself, of being ready to practice self-acceptance.

You could create words to go with the ritual if you like. Perhaps you cross saying, "I am ready to love myself!" And when you reach the other side, your green witch friends greet you with: "We welcome you into the Circle of Love!"

It's then your turn to be one of the witnesses as your friend comes around to the other side of the rose threshold. Remember: it's important not to cross it. Go around it, except when you cross it in the ritual.

When all who are present have crossed the threshold, and been welcomed and shared some hugs and laughter, it's time for a celebration! Share some rose blossom tea and chocolate! Everyone can have a spoonful of rose blossom honey to celebrate the sweetness of love! When you all feel complete, it's time to release the form of the threshold and let your good magic go back to the Earth.

Using a broom, or your hands, have everyone help sweep away the roses in all directions, so they're no longer in a line. The roses now become part of the land where you are. As you do this, thank the roses for helping you open your heart to yourself and others.

Oatstraw

(AVENA SATIVA)
INNER PEACE AND BEAUTY MAGIC

• •

Also known as: oat grass, oat tops, cat grass, oats
Oatstraw says: "Relax. I see your beauty and strength."

Meet Oatstraw

Have you ever seen me
Swaying in the breeze?
With my roots well-planted
I move as I please.
Grasses dancing in place
Whisper my love song
Growing beauty and grace
And nerves that are strong.
I help you stand your ground,
Holding peace within,
All while growing stronger
Nails, hair, and clear skin.
I help you flow with ease,
Adjust to what's new,
Growing flexible yet
Staying true to you.

Herbal Healing

Oatstraw is many herbalists' go-to plant for stress relief, and it's definitely one of mine. Oats are high in the minerals that nourish our nerves and help us adapt to the stresses of our lives. These same minerals also strengthen our musculoskeletal systems, which form the structure of our bodies— our muscles, bones, cartilage, joints, ligaments, sinews, and tendons. These systems are all intertwined, and our nerves run through almost every part of our bodies. Oats can help relieve pain in our joints and muscles, even as they provide relief for "pain" in our minds that may show up as anxiety or depression.

I love that oatstraw is both soothing and strengthening. Think of this plant as a relative who loves you and knows just what to say to help you calm down when you feel anxious or frazzled! I prefer to use the whole plant, meaning the stalks *and* the seeds/tops, because I want to get everything oatstraw has to give me. We get more of the nutritive minerals that help balance our blood sugar, improve our digestion, and strengthen our bones from the whole plant infusion. Whether we are drinking oats or bathing in them, we prepare our medicine with the dried plant.

Working with Oatstraw

This is the only cultivated plant among the wild, weedy ones that populate this guidebook. So why include it? Whether you grow your oats or find wild fields of it in which to forage, this is a supremely helpful and magical herb to get to know. It's one of our most nourishing herbs and tastes great on its own, yet it mixes easily and deliciously into different tea blends. Oatstraw strengthens our bones and digestion, relieves pain, and helps clear our skin. Best of all, the more oatstraw we drink, the more resilient we become!

Oats are easy to grow in a pot or in your garden, and, of course, they are familiar to us as oatmeal. We make our herbal preparations from the grass or "straw" that the seeds grow atop, and also from the fresh, unripe seeds. Oatmeal, on the other hand, is made from the mature, dried seeds of the oat plant. I like to say that oat*straw* is the herbal medicine that tastes much better than it sounds! Though oats aren't officially a "wild" plant, they do easily escape cultivation.

Identifying Oatstraw

Oats are a member of the plant family Poaceae (po-ay-see-ay) or, as it's more commonly called, the grass family. According to the World Resources Institute, grasslands cover more than 40 percent of the Earth, or roughly twenty million square miles. The ecological importance of these grasses goes far beyond our modern obsession with "lawns." Grasses, including oats, hold topsoil in place. Topsoil is precious—we need it to grow our food. The leaves of oats are green and form somewhat of a rosette where they meet the soil, and the seedheads form a loose panicle atop a hollow stem. A panicle is a botanical term for a loose, branching cluster of flowers. Wild oats are usually a darker green than cultivated ones, and oats usually dry to a golden color. All oat leaves have a subtle, counterclockwise twist to them when looked at from above.

The leaves of oats are wider than those of most other cereal grains and typically grow from two to three feet tall.

Gathering Oatstraw

You can harvest oatstraw before or after the seeds are ripe, but it's best to gather this plant before the stalks turn yellow. I grow mine in barrels and harvest them when the tops are "in milk," meaning you can gently squeeze the unripe seeds and see seed milk ooze from them. I gather the entire aboveground portion of the plant. I like to hold the base of the stalk where it meets the earth, and with my other hand, I gently, yet firmly, use a circular twisting motion to disconnect the stalk from the underground portion of the plant, very close to the soil. Or, you can pull the whole plant up and snip off the roots to dry the upper parts by hanging them upside down in small bundles.

Creativity in the Kitchen

Oatstraw is very rich in calcium, silica, B vitamins, iron, and magnesium. It helps balance your blood sugar, improve your digestion, and stabilize your moods. As a bonus, you'll notice clearer skin, stronger nails, and healthier hair! The most helpful way to use oatstraw regularly is also the most basic: as a simple herbal infusion. A "simple" is also an herbalist's term for a medicinal preparation that is made with a single herb.

OATSTRAW INFUSION

|||||||||||||||||||||||||||||||||||||||||||||||||||||||||||||||

Here's the recipe to use oatstraw on a regular basis to become calmer and more at ease in your daily life.

INGREDIENTS:

1 cup dried oatstraw, stalks and tops

1 quart boiling water

DIRECTIONS:

- Put the stalks or stalks and tops into a glass quart jar or a stainless steel or enamel saucepan and pour the boiling water over the dried oats.
- Cover tightly and (depending on the time of day) leave out on the counter to steep overnight, all day, or as long as you can wait! When ready, pour off the liquid through a strainer and squeeze the herbs to get all the milky goodness from the oats. Squeeze them back into the jar of infusion, or into a saucepan if you are going to reheat them. You can drink the herbal infusion at room temperature, or reheat it to drink, and either store it in a thermos to drink throughout the day or refrigerate whatever you are not going to drink until later.

OATSTRAW TEA

||||||||||||||||||||||||||||||||||||||||||||||||||||||||||||||||

When you need stress relief, and just can't wait, it's time to make some oatstraw tea.

Boil approximately 1 tablespoon of dried oatstraw in 8 ounces of water for 3–5 minutes, then turn the flame off, let it steep for 10 more minutes, and drink. By the time you finish your cup of tea, you will be noticeably more relaxed.

OATSTRAW-LEMON BALM SUPER SOOTHER

||||||||||||||||||||||||||||||||||||||||||||||||||||||||||||||||

As I mentioned, oatstraw combines well with many different herbs. The lemon balm adds a wonderful citrus flavor to the brew and enhances the calming effects of the tea, especially soothing tension in the belly. It also adds an uplifting quality to go with the calming effects of oatstraw. You can also make it stronger as a full-strength infusion, if you prefer, by steeping it for hours. Either way, remember to use dried herbs.

INGREDIENTS:

1 quart boiling water

½ cup dried oatstraw

¼–½ cup lemon balm, to taste
(*Melissa officinalis*)

DIRECTIONS:

o Pour boiled water over the herbs inside a teapot or saucepan. Wait about a half hour, then pour through a filter and enjoy!

Here is one of my all-time favorite recipes. I call it my:

PERSONAL SUSTAINABILITY BLEND

This infusion is tasty and provides lots of vitamins and minerals as it builds blood and bone and strengthens your nerves and muscles. Red clover adds to the skin-clearing and mentally calming qualities, and nettles build stamina, increasing your energy and immunity!

INGREDIENTS:

1 quart boiling water

⅓ cup oatstraw

⅓ cup nettles

⅓ cup red clover

DIRECTIONS:

- Pour the boiling water over the herbs in your mason jar or saucepan. Cover tightly and let them steep overnight.
- You can also make a simple tea while you're waiting for your infusion to be ready! Put 2 teaspoons of each herb into a tea ball or other filter and place that in your mug. Cover with boiling water. Steep for 15 minutes or more. Take out your herbs, give them a squeeze, then enjoy your tea.

OATMEAL SCRUB FOR GLOWING SKIN

||||||||||||||||||||||||||||||||||||||||||||||||||||||||||||||

Loosely grind rolled oats in an electric grinder or with a mortar and pestle. Store them in a glass jar in your bathroom. Put some in your hand or in a small bowl to combine with warm water for a gentle exfoliant to stimulate healthy skin on your face and body. When you do this a few times you'll discover which texture you like best, smoother or flakier.

This recipe also combines beautifully with roses. Use about 1 tablespoon of dried roses to 1 cup of rolled oats.

Oatstraw in Magic and Ritual

In the case of oatstraw, her medicine is her magic, and her magic is her medicine. Oatstraw is the plant that best exemplifies one of my favorite magical incantations:

It is enough just to be
It is enough just to be
It is enough just to be

Sometimes, when your mind gets stuck on something uncomfortable, it can feel like you're trapped on a speeding train, with no way to slow down or get off. The answer to how to stop thinking so much is to move your attention and awareness into your body. With the help of oatstraw, this magical, moving meditation will guide you in how to do that.

AN OATSTRAW RITUAL

THIS RITUAL IS BEST DONE OUTDOORS, BAREFOOT. IT CAN BE shared with friends or done on your own. If you can't be outside, stand barefoot on your rug or floor. If music is helpful to you, put some on. Close your eyes and settle into the present.

Relax. Now, imagine you are out in a meadow.

You are a stalk of oat grass, and a soft gentle breeze is blowing. Feel how your body naturally wants to sway in the breeze, and let your flowing breath become the breeze.

Bring your attention down your body and imagine feeling many thin, shallow roots growing from the bottoms of your feet, or from where your feet used to be. Feel those roots reaching down, grasping the Earth, holding tightly to the soil, feeding and being fed by it.

Your grass roots are so strong!

Imagine that over days and nights you are growing taller, and seeds begin to ripen along your stalk. Now you are tall oat grass, top-heavy with milky seeds, swaying and dancing with gentle breezes, or maybe you're being blown about by wild winds.

The winds may even flatten you against the ground, but you spring back up again. Feel yourself dancing with the winds of change as beautiful, flowing oat grass, your roots anchored in the Earth, holding and supporting you.

When you're ready, imagine the air getting calmer, growing still, inviting your oat grass stalk body to come to center, to stillness. Draw your roots back up until they become feet that are free to go anywhere again as you regain your human shape, feeling more fluid and connected than before, with the blessing of Avena, oatstraw.

Here is another oatstraw ritual that I know you will enjoy.

SWEET AND SOOTHING OATSTRAW-LAVENDER BATH

|||||||||||||||||||||||||||||||||||||||||||||||||||||||||||||

INGREDIENTS:

1½–2½ cups dried oatstraw

Half gallon or gallon of cold water

¼ cup dried lavender flowers

DIRECTIONS:

- Put the oatstraw into a half gallon or gallon of cold water in a soup pot.
- Bring the water to a boil, then cover the pot and turn it down to simmer on the lowest possible flame for about 30 minutes.
- Turn it off and stir in the dried lavender flowers.
- Cover the pot and wait another 30–60 minutes.
- Pour the strained infusion into a full bath.

- Hum for a few minutes as you lie in the bath and feel how the vibration moves through your bones. Or you could put on some music you love.
- Let the magic of these herbs bring you to a peaceful place, quieting your mind, soothing your heart, and on top of all that, beautifying your skin.

Violet
(*VIOLA ODORATA*)
SOOTHING HEART MAGIC

• •

Also known as: sweet blue violet, heartsease, Johnny jump-up
Violet says: "Open your heart. You are strong enough to be gentle."

Meet Violet

Violet teaches
But never preaches
She melts hot rage
So you turn the page
To find new peace
Relief and release
Softens your heart
When it's torn apart
If you are mad
She won't say that's bad
If you must cry
Violet won't ask why
She helps tears flow
So you can let go.

Herbal Healing

The essence of violet is found in her sweetness and her ability to get feelings that are "stuck" moving again. Violet magically helps return us to a natural state of joy. In the body, violet strengthens the nervous system so we're more resilient. Whether it's a hot, dry cough or a hot, inflamed temper, violet's cool gifts make her a powerful ally to get to know.

This lovely little plant helps our feelings flow and helps us physically by supporting the flow of lymph fluid throughout the lymphatic system.

You have a wondrous circulatory system throughout your entire body consisting of thick arteries that carry blood from your heart to all your organs and tissues, and thinner veins that bring the blood back again to your heart and lungs to receive fresh oxygen before returning to the arteries and making the trip around your body again. There is another circulatory system whose vessels live alongside your blood vessels called your lymphatic system. It's filled with special fluid called lymph that helps your body protect itself against infections. Your lymph forms a major component of your immune system.

Among herbalists and everyday people all over the world who still rely on herbs for medicine, violet is famous for soothing and relieving physical and emotional pain.

I like to use violet for stress headaches, especially ones that come from overthinking or from when you are frustrated and angry about something or someone. Interestingly, violet is high in salicylic acid, the component chemists studied to develop a common headache and pain reliever—aspirin.

Working with Violet

The violet family (Violaceae) is a large one that contains many species. In the northeastern United States alone there are fifty-two species, so there will be distinct variations in how they look. Violets are generally low plants that tend to grow in the shade (or, at least, they are happiest there), and the leaves are cool to the touch and moist when you break them open. If you rub them briskly between your hands, they are very juicy, even slimy.

Violets help awaken your outer and inner senses when you engage with these delightful beings. As their nickname—"heartsease"—suggests, violets will gently melt away hardness that may have grown around your heart and elsewhere in the body physically, such as by softening and dissolving stuck gunk in the lungs or bronchi that can cause a harsh cough.

It's a pleasure to engage with violets on any level. These humble plants are easy to overlook when they aren't flowering, and impossible to ignore when they are. Their blossoms are so beautiful and exuberant! In fact, sweet blue violet is the plant so in love with life that she flowers twice—once just for fun, and once to set seeds. Violet remains close to the earth at all stages of her growth and exudes a gentle energy. Whether you are sitting with a plant, sharing breath in the connection ritual, gathering leaves for food or herbal medicine, or even simply gazing at or sketching a patch of violets, your thoughts will inevitably grow more serene. What a gift!

Identifying Violet

Wild violets often have heart-shaped leaves and two sets of flowers: first come the famous purple ones with their irregular shape of four upswept petals and one longer petal facing downward. There are also violet species that have the same heart-shaped leaves, but have lighter-colored flowers—lavender, purple with white stripes, and all white. All species can spread abundantly through gardens and wild meadows. Each flower grows on a single, hairless stalk, just as the dark green, heart-shaped leaves do.

The coolest thing about most wild violet species is that their leaves curl inward a little bit, the edges are rolled closed, and they always look like they are just about to unfurl and open.

It makes me think of how we hunch over sometimes, as if to protect our hearts by closing them off. We open them when and where we feel safe. The second set of flowers is the reproductive flowers, which are green and much less showy. They grow on their own shorter stalks in late summer and fall and lie down on the ground underneath the leaves. You have to look closely to find them. When they grow into seed pods, they open in three parts, looking like a starry pea pod full of green pearls! These are very beautiful.

Gathering Violets

We collect the familiar, purple flowers (or any of the other wild violet flowers) in the early part of the spring and harvest the leaves at any time before there is a frost. Violets can be gathered from the wild or grown in your garden. I like to do both. One of the great things about gathering wild weeds is that there are usually plenty! Violet grows in all but the driest of places. I've picked some of the best violets from rich, muddy streambeds in the woods. Don't forget to ask permission and give thanks before gathering. As long as you've received a "yes" and there are enough violets, you may gather leaves and/or flowers from whichever of these violets are growing in that one area.

Use two hands, one to hold the plant close to the earth and the other to pinch off the stalk with the leaf or flower attached, as close to the ground as you can get.

I don't recommend washing the leaves, unless they are actually dirty or gritty, like after a heavy rain if dirt has splashed up onto them. It is better to pick them carefully and cleanly, perhaps brushing them off gently with your hand if needed.

Put your violets into a paper bag or basket to bring them home to dry. Lay them out on screens or wicker trays, or even paper towels in a pinch, out of direct sunlight, and so they're not touching each other if possible. You'll know they are dry and ready to be put away when you bend them and they crack. Place them in a clean, dry paper bag and label it with both the common and botanical name of the plant, and the month, year, and place of your harvest. Store your bag in a cool, dry place that has at least some ventilation.

Creativity in the Kitchen

You can make many wonderful herbal preparations with both fresh violets and the leaves you've dried! Let's start with a poultice. A poultice is what an herbal preparation is called when we lay fresh or dried herbs directly onto the skin anywhere on the body.

TO USE FRESH VIOLETS TOPICALLY (EXTERNALLY): Roll one or more fresh, clean leaves between your palms to gently open the cell walls of the plant and release violet's cooling, soothing moisture. Place one or more fresh leaves on your body. For example, to help with a headache, lay them at the nape of your neck, where it meets your skull. Press them against your skin gently and they will stick there. You can also just lick the whole leaf and it will stick well, too. Or, you can splash a touch of warm water onto them first, then place them on your neck. Place another leaf (or several leaves) onto your forehead. Close your eyes and sit and breathe quietly. Relax into the present moment with violet and feel how the pain diminishes and tension is eased.

Dried violet leaves can also be used. Simply take enough violets for the area you wish to cover with your poultice. Place the dried herbs into a cup or bowl and pour just enough boiling water over them to cover. Soak the herbs for 5–10 minutes, then remove them from the water. Use a fork or tongs since the water will still be hot. The leaves will cool quickly once removed from the water, so when they are comfortable to handle, squeeze them a bit to remove excess water so they won't drip, then proceed with your poultice as described above.

You can increase the effectiveness of violet medicine by drinking it. Make a delicious violet leaf or leaf-and-flower infusion and drink it hot, room temperature, or even iced if you prefer! It's best to use dried violets, as the preparation will be both more flavorful and more potent.

VIOLET LEAF OR LEAF-AND-FLOWER INFUSION

INGREDIENTS:
1 cup dried violet leaves (or leaves and flowers)
1 quart boiling water
Honey, to taste (optional)

DIRECTIONS:

- Put the leaves into a 1-quart jar or saucepan and pour the boiling water over the herbs. Cover tightly and leave out on the counter to steep for an hour. When ready, pour off the liquid and squeeze the herbs to get all the goodness from the violets. You can reheat the infusion to drink and/or refrigerate whatever you're not going to use right away. **OR:**
- To make a simple tea by the cup, put about 2–3 tablespoons of violet leaves in a tea ball strainer. Place that in your favorite mug, pour boiling water over the herbs, and let them sit, steeping for 15 minutes or so, covered with a little plate. You can add honey to taste if you like.

VIOLET FLOWER ICE CUBES

Remove fresh violet flowers from their stalks. Fill an ice cube tray with water, leaving room to add one or two flowers to each square. Freeze to make ice cubes, as usual. When they are frozen, you have beautiful ice cubes to add to a glass of water.

SWEET VIOLET-MUSHROOM- CHEESE OMELET

INGREDIENTS:

Butter, for cooking, as needed

½ cup chopped red onion

½ cup sliced shiitake or other mushrooms

½ cup chopped fresh violet leaves

½ teaspoon dried rosemary

2 eggs

2 tablespoons water, milk, or yogurt,
plus some extra water for cooking

Cheddar cheese, grated

5–10 fresh violet flowers (if available)

Salt and pepper, to taste (optional)

DIRECTIONS:

- Melt the butter in a stainless steel, enamel, or cast-iron fry pan.
- Add the chopped onions. Cover and cook them until they are soft and translucent, about 10 minutes. Stir as needed.
- Add the mushrooms and cook for 3–5 minutes, stirring as needed, then add the violet leaves and the dried rosemary. If needed, add extra water little by little to keep the ingredients from sticking to the pan or burning.
- Cover and cook for another 5 minutes while you crack the eggs into a bowl, adding the water, milk, or yogurt to make the omelet even fluffier.
- Beat the eggs very well, then pour them over the vegetables and herbs in the pan. Make sure the flame is on medium or low, not high.
- When the omelet is set in a few short minutes, add the grated cheese on top and turn off the flame. Cover and wait a few minutes for the cheese to melt.
- Fold the omelet in half with a spatula, place the flowers on top for their beauty as well as taste, and serve hot, adding salt and/or pepper to taste if desired. Enjoy!

Violet in Magic and Ritual

Violet is powerful and yet a bit shy. She gently melts away resistance and helps us express our grief, too.

Violet can help you heal difficult relationships by showing you the hidden sweetness in someone you are having difficulty with. It sounds hard to believe, but I've seen it many times, and I must confess, I don't know exactly how it works, but that's the nature of magic—it's mysterious! Nevertheless, here's one of the ways I think about it: when you are outside gathering violet leaves, they don't have a strong scent, but when you put your nose into a bag or right up close to the green leaves, the scent is subtle but swoon-worthy. Violet herself has hidden sweetness. When we take her into ourselves, she helps us find that same sweetness in others.

Perhaps there is a grown-up or classmate you find it really tough to be around. Maybe they're crabby and mean, or they're rude and talk down to you. And yet, you have to see them frequently. If you're tired of tensing up around them, and you can open your mind to the possibility that it might make *your* life easier to find some sweetness in them, and might even *possibly* change how they behave toward you, try drinking violet tea as a ritual. Violet's ability to awaken our kindness and compassion makes us feel better.

Make a quart of violet leaf and/or flower tea or infusion. Drink anywhere from a tablespoon to one-fourth cup every day for nine days. Every time you drink the sweet violet tea, you can add a magical invocation. In this case, you might say, "I'm open to seeing _____ through the eyes of my heart."

Be open to the magical possibilities!

INVOCATION

An invocation is a magical incantation used for calling something into being. It is a spell, and it's a green witch's version of a mantra. "Mantra" comes from a Sanskrit word meaning a "sacred message or text, charm, spell, or counsel." An invocation is something magical you chant or say over and over again to help something come into being, or that you can use as an affirmation to help you remember something that is true, like "I deserve love and happiness."

You could also put dried violet leaves in a little cotton bag (muslin or silk fabrics are nice, too, if easy for you to find), and carry it with you in your pocket or in a little pouch around your neck.

Here is a lovely, magical practice you can do with the help of violets to soothe and calm yourself when you feel sad or angry (or just because it feels good): Lie down or sit somewhere you feel safe and comfortable and won't be disturbed. Place the leaves and/or flowers over your heart center.

Violet will soothe your heart. Whether you feel sad or angry, violet will gently help you feel what you feel. If you need to cry and haven't been able to, or you just need to cry some more, violet will help you release those tears so you can find relief. As you know, it's so painful when you shut down your heart against yourself, or against someone you care about. Picture a hard casing around your heart that you placed there for self-protection. Imagine that hard case softening, little by little, until it's melted away. Do this visualization as many times as you need to. Violet doesn't push, but helps you open your heart when you are ready.

A VIOLET RITUAL

VIOLET MELTS AWAY ALL THAT STANDS IN THE WAY OF LOVE. And love is a powerful force. It can be fierce if needed: think of a mother bear taking a threatening stance to protect her cubs. It can also be as gentle as a new parent holding their baby in their arms. Violet will open you to the power of your own heart and help you find ways to express the love inside you.

Use this magical exercise as a way to access the infinite power of love, and as a way to access and activate your deeper intuitive vision.

Sit or lie in a comfortable place where it's quiet (you can put on some instrumental music if that helps you relax). Lick a whole fresh violet leaf and place it on your forehead over your third eye with the point of the heart just between your eyebrows.

The third eye (I call it our first eye) is the spiritual eye of insight, the eye that sees true. We perceive with our inner vision through this magical eye, and with it we can see the beauty that is always present when we are open to see it.

Relax your breathing and become aware of whatever you are feeling. Just let yourself be. An invocation you can say to yourself is: "I am opening my heart." Or "I am strong enough to be gentle." Or perhaps "I am strong enough to be vulnerable." (All of these are among your superpowers, by the way.)

Hang out with that for awhile. Then, if you feel like going further, you can ask for and thank Violet for helping you awaken your truest vision so that more and more often, you will be able to see yourself and others through the eyes of your strong, tender heart.

After you rise, write or draw in your green witch journal to record anything you felt or that came up in your thoughts; even wispy images or fragments of an idea may lead to new insights. It's okay if you're not totally sure what they mean to you yet. Writing or sketching to get some things down on paper will help you reflect on your experience in the moment, and you may realize different things when you reread it any time later. Writing down your thoughts and feelings is an important part of the ritual, and the act of doing that can help you make sense of ideas that your intuition awakens in you. Also, you may be surprised to notice your own growth when you read back over your green witch journal weeks or months later.

Motherwort

(*LEONURUS CARDIACA*)
COURAGE AND LION-HEARTED MAGIC

· ·

Also known as: lion's ear, lion's tail, mother's herb
Motherwort says: "You are braver than you think, and
I bring comfort when you need it."

Meet Motherwort

I know I taste bitter
Of that there's no doubt,
But I bring you courage
That's what I'm about.
I soothe anxiety
And gladden your heart,
I relieve any cramps
And that's just the start!
It's said that I bestow
Immortality,
Though that's just a legend
I'll help you to be . . .
Calmer and braver
And happier, too,
When you get to know me
You'll see it's all true!

Herbal Healing

Motherwort is a plant that brings healing to both the emotional and physical heart. It tones the nervous and cardiovascular systems and smooths out fast or irregular heartbeat rhythms.

A healthy heart is all about rhythm. Your nervous system controls how many times your heart beats per minute. It beats more slowly when you are resting and faster when you are running, dancing, or playing.

We all sometimes need help with anxiety and tension, as well as with muscular cramps. Though best known as a calming plant, motherwort can also be used as a bitter, which is an important category of herbs that strengthen our digestion. Motherwort's bitterness and stomach-relaxing effects can help to relieve constipation that's caused by stress.

Most people feel motherwort's calming effects almost instantaneously. For acute, in-the-moment nervousness or anxiety—perhaps on your first day in a new school, or trying out for a part in a play—motherwort is one of the best remedies ever!

Working with Motherwort

Motherwort is truly one of my most highly valued herbs. She is the first one I reach for to relieve anxiety quickly. This essential plant ally soothes our emotions and strengthens our hearts.

The botanical name, *Leonurus cardiaca*, translates as "the lion-hearted one." This wild plant is a member of the Lamiaceae family, more commonly known as the mint family. This is a *very* large family of plants, ranging from plants like the oregano you enjoy on your pizza, to the lemon-flavored *Melissa officinalis*/lemon balm from the oatstraw chapter, to the lavender that we'll get to soon! Almost all mints share certain properties—they are helpful to our digestion, rich in oils that give these plants their wonderful (or at least strong) aromas, and high in antioxidants that support our overall health through protecting our hearts and improving circulation.

Identifying Motherwort

Motherwort likes moist, fertile soil and a little shade, and grows abundantly along the edges of woods, as a weed in the garden, in open fields, in meadows and vacant lots, and just about anywhere except in the deepest shade or brightest sun.

The plants tend to grow in dense clusters, and though motherwort is said to have originated in southern Russia and Eurasia, it is now naturalized all over the world, where it is valued as one of the great herbal medicines, or dismissed as an invasive weed, depending on who's looking!

Growing up to five feet tall and flowering from June through September, the flowers are pink to pale purple and appear in clusters rising along the stem, growing out of sepals that become prickly as they start to produce seeds.

Like all mint family plants, motherwort has opposite leaves on square stems—though not all square-stemmed plants are mints. The leaves alternate going up the stem and totally change shape from the bottom of the plant to the top! They start out large and maple-like, which in botany is called "palmate"—like the palm of your hand, but they get narrower and narrower as they reach the top, and especially when the plant flowers.

Plants like motherwort wisely "choose" to put their energy where it's most needed in whatever cycle of life they are in. It's common for a plant's upper leaves to get smaller when the flowers need more of the plant's energy so they can produce nectar for the pollinators and seeds for the next generations.

The taller this perennial plant grows, the more obviously square the stalks become. The stalks are hollow inside, and all parts of the plant are covered with tiny hairs, including the bitter-tasting flowers.

Motherwort has a distinctive scent and taste, but this one is not particularly "minty"—instead it is quite bitter! You can investigate this for yourself by rubbing a leaf briskly between your hands, then sniffing it.

Gathering Motherwort

It is best to gather motherwort when the plant is in flower, and before the sepals become too prickly. This plant has quite a powerful presence, and though the leaves change markedly from the bottom of the plant to the top, we can use them all. Motherwort often has a main, thick stalk, and many smaller ones branching off of that. If you're gathering from the central stalk, I suggest gathering the upper third or so, harvesting the stalks, leaves, and flowers. However, if you gather the smaller flowering stalks that are branching off the main stalk, motherwort will generally give them to you more easily when you are using your hands, which I always suggest you do, rather than scissors or a knife. The plant appreciates this so much, and you learn to feel where the plant wants to give itself to you. Please remember that it is also easier for you to gather the flowering stalks before they get too prickly. This is a very generous plant who shares abundantly and radiates a soothing, calming effect.

Creativity in the Kitchen

Motherwort doesn't lend herself to strong infusions because of those bitter, volatile oils; so a simple tea will be likelier to help, mainly because you'll be more likely to drink it!

MOTHERWORT TEA

||||||||||||||||||||||||||||||||||||||||||||||||||||||||||||||||||

INGREDIENTS:

1 teaspoon dried motherwort leaves (or leaves and flowers)

8 ounces boiling water

Honey, to taste (optional)

DIRECTIONS:

○ Put the dried motherwort into a stainless steel filter/sieve or tea ball, and pour the boiled water over it. Steep covered for about 15 minutes before removing the herbs and drinking your tea.

○ Note that the bitter taste of motherwort is part of what makes it such an effective helper, and you might be surprised to learn that oftentimes when we actually need something, it will taste good to us, whereas at other times it may not. Having said all this, if you need to sweeten your tea to make it easier to drink, add a bit of honey.

MOTHERWORT-INFUSED VINEGAR

||||||||||||||||||||||||||||||||||||||||||||||||||||||||||||||||

You can also infuse your motherwort in apple cider vinegar. This makes a tasty medicine that you can spoon into water and use similarly to the tea. Also, this way it is conveniently ready for you to use whenever you need it, and it will last for quite a long time (at least one year).

INGREDIENTS:

Flowering motherwort, enough to almost fill a 1-pint jar

1 pint apple cider vinegar

DIRECTIONS:

○ Chop up the motherwort, and fill the jar almost to the top.

○ Pour in the apple cider vinegar until it reaches the top of the jar. (If you only have a metal lid, be sure to line it with unbleached wax or parchment paper to prevent the lid from rusting closed. Plastic wrap works, too, but I prefer paper.)

○ Poke the herbs down under the vinegar with whatever utensil you have handy.

- Cap the jar with a plastic lid or a cork that tightly seals.
- Label and keep your jar in a cool, dry place. It will be ready in 2–4 weeks. Taste and smell it and decide when you want to decant it.
- Decant it by pouring the liquid through a strainer, then squeeze out the herbs as thoroughly as you can, either in your hands or in a thin cloth like cheesecloth or muslin. Compost your herbs, and your vinegar is ready!
- When you don't have fresh motherwort available, you can use the dried plant to make your vinegar. Follow the recipe above but instead of filling the jar to the top, fill it ⅓ full with the dried herbs. Shake this preparation every few days or so to help the herbs infuse more fully into the vinegar.
- You can also experiment with using the quick vinegar method described in the rose section, on page 26.

MOTHERWORT-INFUSED OIL

||||||||||||||||||||||||||||||||||||||||||||||||||||||||||||||||||

INGREDIENTS:

Fresh motherwort, enough to fill your wide-mouth jar almost to the top
Olive oil (use cold-pressed olive oil, preferably from a glass bottle or a can)

DIRECTIONS:

- Gather fresh motherwort leaves or a combination of leaves, small stalks, and flowers.
- Do not wash the leaves, as that will make your oil get moldy.
- Rip or cut up the plant into small pieces measuring about ½ inch.
- Place them into a completely dry, wide-mouth jar, packing it almost to the top.

continued

- Cover with olive oil, using a stick or utensil of some sort to make space while you pour the oil so all the plant material gets fully saturated. When it's full to the top, continue to poke down to the bottom of your jar for a couple of minutes, and you'll see air bubbles floating to the top.
- You want to release/pop as many of them as you can so moisture won't get trapped inside the jar.
- Cover your jar and label it. This preparation will not need to be shaken, but it is wise to put it on a plate or sit it in a bowl because the plant *will* continue to release air bubbles, and they may cause the oil to spill over the sides of your jar. For the first week or two, it's good to open the jar now and then and poke down the plant material to make sure it's all covered with olive oil, and add a bit more if necessary.
- When you pour off the oil, and squeeze out the leaves, wait one day. Then, slowly pour out all but the last ¼ inch or so of oil in the jar, put your decanted oil into a fresh jar, and use the original oil first as it will be a bit watery.
- It will be ready to be decanted in 2–4 weeks and will make a lovely, soothing oil that will be helpful for relaxation and muscle cramps.

Motherwort in Magic and Ritual

Motherwort's magic is like a soothing touch to your heart.

Here is a simple, yet powerful, ritual for when you are feeling anxious about something. It could be a situation at home or maybe a test at school or a big game. Maybe you and a friend had an argument. Whatever it is, let this ritual reassure you.

A MOTHERWORT RITUAL

SIT WITH A MOTHERWORT PLANT.

I encourage you to touch the plant, and imagine your heart and motherwort's heart beginning to beat together. You might put your hands over your heart now. Talk to motherwort silently or aloud, and tell her anything you are feeling about something you wish were different than it is!

Then, ask her to help you learn how to trust the bitter as well as the sweet.

Ask her for one leaf.

When she gives you permission, gently take the leaf and nibble a little bit of it.

Motherwort is kind and loving, and she knows how to digest life's bitter parts and will help you do the same. Think about how you might feel if you weren't fighting with what is. Know that as you take her bitterness into yourself, you are letting life know that you at least *want* to trust it, and are doing your best. Trust that motherwort will help you. Because she always will.

Note: If you don't have a plant to sit with, purchase a little dried motherwort from an herb shop and place it on a pretty plate or bowl. You can set that on an altar cloth to create a sacred space. Then do the same ritual, knowing the living essence of the motherwort is still there in the dried plant. You can either nibble the dried plant, or take her into you as tea.

Artemisia/Mugwort

(*ARTEMISIA VULGARIS*)
INTUITION AND DREAM BIG MAGIC

• •

Also known as: cronewort, sailor's tobacco, chrysanthemum weed
Artemisia says: "Trust yourself and be true to yourself!"

Meet Artemisia/Mugwort

I am a goddess
And also a weed
And you each have wisdom
I'll teach you to heed
I have a talent
For helping you know
That turning within
Will guide you to grow

My leaves are two-toned
One side green, one gray
I love the Sun and Moon
And help you to say
What is on your mind
And in your heart too
As you confidently
Express what is true

Herbal Healing

It is said that the silver undersides reveal a secret: this plant is connected to the Moon and all things lunar, such as intuition and the tides of the oceans.

Did you know that our word "month" comes from root words that mean "Moon" and "to measure"—as in measuring cycles of time by the phases of the Moon?

This plant offers healing for the entire body. Artemisia is high in vitamins and minerals and aids digestion, strengthens the nerves, sharpens the mind, and helps build strong bones and flexible joints. This plant is also valuable as an herb to use in a homemade steam bath for bronchitis or asthma. You might need a parent to help you with this one, at least the first time.

Working with Artemisia/Mugwort

Most people call this plant "mugwort," and one explanation is that it's the herb that fills the mug (it was often used for brewing beer). A green witch named

Susun Weed, who has written many herbal medicine books, renamed this herb "cronewort," and that name has become very popular.

> The word for an old woman, "crone," comes from the Greek name Cronus, which means "time." Crone was once a term of deep respect, then it became an insult, and now it's slowly but surely returning to its rightful place of honor—as a title that speaks to the wisdom of elder women, the wisdom of our grandmothers.

I prefer to call this plant by her botanical name, Artemisia, for this plant is said to be sacred to the maiden goddess Artemis, and so was named for her.

There are many myths about the Greek goddess Artemis. She is both fierce and kind, sometimes seen as dangerous to approach, yet she is a protectress of mothers-to-be and the wild creatures of the woodlands. Like most goddesses she is known by many different names, depending on who is telling her story and what part of the world they hail from. In Italy, she is called Diana, the huntress.

When we come into a relationship with the plant Artemisia in teas, baths, oils, and magical rituals, it's as if Artemis herself comes and teaches us to be attuned to our inner voice and to be true to ourselves. She doesn't want us to be indoors too much either. She is an outdoor goddess, always connected to the forest, and in the same way, *Artemisia vulgaris*/mugwort, wild weed that she is, would not be happy in a pot indoors. She might grow for you, but that setting would be against her true nature, so go outside and you will find her almost anywhere you live.

However, fresh or dried sprigs or branches in a vase could be a perfect way to bring this goddess of a plant indoors while still respecting her wild nature.

Identifying Artemisia/Mugwort

This plant grows abundantly in disturbed soils, rocky ground, and cultivated garden beds. In other words, mugwort is not picky, though it does prefer sunshine to shade.

Artemisia starts off in the spring with tiny leaves poking up from under the earth, and, by the end of the growing season, the plant can have achieved heights of six feet or more and have thick, woody, and often hairy stalks. The deeply lobed leaves that are close to the soil and continue up the stalk will become slender little rays by the time they reach the top of the flowering stalks.

Artemisia is a member of a huge plant family known as the Asteraceae, or the daisy family. But unlike daisies, whose showy flowers you can't miss, you'll need a magnifying glass to fully appreciate the extraordinary beauty of the tiny yellow and green flowers that grow on mugwort's upper stalks.

Sometimes they are described in field guides as "insignificant" flowers, but they are a food source for butterflies and moths! They are pollinated mostly by the wind, but also by a variety of bees and flies.

One of the most outstanding characteristics you will observe about *Artemisia vulgaris* is that the leaves are olive or dark green on top and silver-white and downy underneath.

These potent plants are aromatic and call for engaging the senses beyond just looking at them. When you rub the leaves between your fingers, mugwort plants exude a distinctive, camphory, bitter scent.

Gathering Artemisia/Mugwort

In the spring, gather the small leaves, including the soft, flexible stalks on which they grow. In summer, gather the maturing leaves, along with the still-soft stalks they are growing on. I always especially look forward to the late summer and fall when mugwort goes into flower. Now the stalks are quite woody, and you can snap them about one-third of the way down to gather the entire aboveground parts of the plants for magic, or pick off only the tiny flowers for especially potent magical preparations. Always look carefully at the undersides of the plants since so many insects love Artemisia.

Creativity in the Kitchen

In cultures around the world, especially in Asia and Europe, Artemisia's leaves are used in cooking. As a bitter digestive aid, this plant can help with digesting fats such as those found in meat and chicken.

In the spring, when mugwort's leaves are tiny and tender, you can chop and add them raw to salads. Later in the summer, you can pick a couple inches off the tops of the plant and put them into sandwiches, or cook them in your eggs or add to soups!

ARTEMISIA/MUGWORT STEAM BATH

||||||||||||||||||||||||||||||||||||||||||||||||||||||||

**PLEASE MAKE THIS PREPARATION
WHEN AN ADULT IS PRESENT TO HELP YOU.**

Put a handful of dried Artemisia in a soup pot. Put a few inches of water in the pot. Cover and bring it to a boil. Turn it off and place the pot on a mat on the table, where you'll be able to sit comfortably and lean over the pot. Take the lid off the pot to let it cool a bit, then put a large towel over your head and the pot and breathe in the steam to relieve a cough. And a side benefit is it'll make your skin feel silky smooth!

ARTEMISIA/MUGWORT TEA

||||||||||||||||||||||||||||||||||||||||||||||||||||||||||||||

Artemisia tea is a nourishing tonic that benefits your whole body and magically helps you come to know and be your true self!

INGREDIENTS:

¼ cup dried Artemisia leaves (or leaves, stalks, and flowers)

DIRECTIONS:

- Put the dried Artemisia into a 1-quart jar.
- Cover with boiling water. Cap. Let steep 30 minutes (longer is fine, too).
- Pour off the liquid and squeeze out the herbs, and it's ready to drink.

ARTEMISIA/MUGWORT & CHAMOMILE BELLY BLISS TEA

||||||||||||||||||||||||||||||||||||||||||||||||||||||||||||||

This tea will soothe bloating and help with stomachaches and indigestion. You can drink it before or after a meal, or really anytime. If you drink it in the evening, it will stimulate your dreams.

INGREDIENTS:

1 teaspoon artemisia leaves

1 tablespoon chamomile flowers

DIRECTIONS:

- Place the ingredients in a mug and cover with boiling water. Let steep for 10–15 minutes.

SPRINGTIME STIR-FRY
WITH ARTEMISIA/MUGWORT

‖‖

Here's a simple recipe that can be eaten as is, or you could add other vegetables or perhaps slices of chicken or tempeh, if you like.

INGREDIENTS:

Sesame oil

1 medium yellow onion, sliced

2 cloves garlic (diced or pressed)

1 medium carrot, sliced

Water, as needed

1 cup fresh or frozen string beans, cut in half or thirds

½ cup fresh flat or curly parsley, chopped (or 1 tablespoon dried)

⅓ cup fresh spring Artemisia leaves, chopped finely

1 teaspoon ginger, grated

Tamari or shoyu, to taste

Rice vinegar, to taste

Salt, to taste

DIRECTIONS:

- Heat sesame oil in a stainless steel or cast-iron fry pan.
- Add the onion and garlic.
- Sauté, covered, for about 10 minutes.
- Stir in the sliced carrots and add water as needed.
- Cover and cook on medium heat for another 10 minutes.
- Stir in the string beans, parsley, Artemisia leaves, and ginger.
- Add a splash of tamari or shoyu and a splash of rice vinegar.
- Cook for another 5–10 minutes.
- Add salt to taste.
- Enjoy!

Artemisia/Mugwort in Magic and Ritual

Artemisia/mugwort stimulates dreams and awakens your intuition or inner wisdom. Mugwort gets stronger as she ages, and though she is *always* magical, she is at her *most* magical when in flower.

ARTEMISIA/MUGWORT RITUALS FOR INNER VISION

FIRST, LET ME SAY THAT I AM USING THE WORD "VISION" BROADLY because not everyone sees images. You might, or instead you might hear an inner voice offering guidance, or you might feel sensations in your body, or maybe you get an emotional feeling. It takes time to learn how your inner voice communicates with you. Continue to explore. Be patient, open-minded, and open-hearted. This is so worth your time!

Sit somewhere you won't be disturbed.

Take a fresh *Artemisia vulgaris* leaf, lick it, and place it on your first eye, between and just above your eyebrows.

Now, close your eyes and ask the plant, or perhaps the wise old crone who lives inside you, no matter your gender or age, to send you a vision of guidance. You might ask a specific question about something you want insight into, or you can simply ask: *What is something it will be helpful for me to know right now? Or to think about?* You can set a timer for at least 5 minutes, or just sit until you feel complete. It is always helpful to write in your green witch journal after sitting, even if you're not sure you "got" anything. If you're with one or more other green witches, write or draw before you talk about what you heard. If there is a supportive older person handy, especially another green witch, you might ask them to sit in your circle sometimes to help you understand anything you saw or felt.

True messages from the spirit of the plants will always be supportive and positive. Truthful guidance is *always* going to be loving and supportive.

AN ARTEMISIA RITUAL FOR DREAMS

Artemisia is famous both for stimulating dreams and helping remember them. Having even one tiny piece of a dream is like having a map to seeing something more.

DIRECTIONS:

○ Put about ½ cup of dried Artemisia leaves in a little bag. You can use a plain bag, or you could sew or glue decorations on it. Put it on or under your pillow, or hang it on a bedpost while you sleep. Ask Artemisia to send you a healing dream, or a dream teaching you something wonderful about yourself. Or you can ask for clarity about a question you have. Sometimes, it is easier to quiet our minds when we are asleep than when we are awake.

○ Keep a journal next to you so that you can write or draw as soon as possible after opening your eyes.

○ If you have trouble remembering your dreams, be patient.

TIP: If you wake up remembering your dream, but on rolling over to pick up your green witch journal you find you've forgotten it, lie down again and put your head with the same part leaning against your pillow. This can sometimes stimulate the return of the memory of the dream!

Lavender

(*LAVANDULA SPP.*)
SWEET BLESSINGS MAGIC

· ·

Also known as: common lavender, spike lavender, garden lavender
Lavender says: "Open to sweet delight!"

Meet Lavender

I'm known to be sweet
But that's not all
If you feel hurt
I'm here when you call
I whisper blessings
Into your ears
Here's my message
To take away fears
You will be OK
I promise you
You're held in love
This really is true

Drink me iced or hot
At any time
To relax and
'Cause I taste sublime
I help you sleep and
Have sweet dreams
I dispel nightmares
And sparkle moon beams
In a sleep pillow
Or in your bath
I'll help you feel
Delight on your path!

Herbal Healing

Lavender can be prepared and used in so many different ways, from a simple, calming tea to stronger infusions for a cleansing ritual. Dried lavender can add a touch of magic to ceremonies and celebratory events such as birthday parties, or it can help you sleep well and enjoy sweet dreams.

Lavender makes a wonderful, effective wash for burns and is used in baths to promote calmness. Infusing lavender in honey is not only yummy to eat, it's a marvelous preparation to have on hand for healing wounds to the skin and preventing infections! This is one powerful plant!

Working with Lavender

Lavender is indigenous to the mountainous regions of the Mediterranean, along with plants such as rosemary and thyme. Although lavender can sometimes be found elsewhere in the wild, this is one that you will most likely need to plant, either outside in a pot or directly into your garden soil, or in a pot on a sunny windowsill indoors.

Lavender is beloved the world over and is also used as a potpourri or a sachet herb to put in a drawer or closet. It helps to repel moths.

But in terms of herbal medicine, lavender is especially famous for promoting calmness and restful sleep. Both the flowers and leaves can be used in herbal medicine, magic, and ritual, though the flowers are usually the preferred part.

The name lavender is derived from a Latin word, *lavare*, which means to wash. In medieval and Renaissance Europe, washerwomen were known as "lavenders" because they spread their laundry over lavender bushes to dry for the scent it gave.

Identifying Lavender

This plant is part of the Lamiaceae (mint) family and can spread to become a small, branching shrub. If you feel the stalk with your fingers, you'll find that any species of lavender has square stems. The leaves are simple and gray-green in color and are about one to two inches long, while the lavender or blue-colored flowers grow on long shoots or spikes that can be eight to sixteen inches long. Lavender prefers dry, sandy soil and grows best in full sun.

Gathering Lavender

It's easy to gather lavender. When the flowers are blooming, and the scent is filling the air, after you've offered your give-away and asked for and received permission to harvest, gather entire flower stalks. You can also harvest leaf stalks after the flowering season is over.

I like to gather the flowers in the summer and the leaves and stalks later in the fall.

Creativity in the Kitchen

Cooking with lavender offers a special treat to the senses! Let's start with preparing an aromatic tea.

LAVENDER TEA/INFUSION

INGREDIENTS:

2 teaspoons dried lavender flowers

DIRECTIONS:

- Put the lavender flowers into a 1-pint jar.
- Cover with boiling water and cap the jar.
- Steep for 5 minutes for tea or 20 minutes for medicinal-strength infusion.

*For an uplifting, delicious variation, you can make one of my favorite teas, lavender-rose. Simply use 1 teaspoon each of lavender and dried red or pink roses!

LAVENDER BUTTER

Try this delicious butter on French toast, pancakes, waffles, or toast!

INGREDIENTS:

½ cup butter
2–2½ teaspoons fresh or dried lavender flowers

DIRECTIONS:

- Melt the butter.
- Stir in lavender flowers.
- Store the mixture in the refrigerator until cool.

LAVENDER HONEY

|||||||||||||||||||||||||||||||||||||||||||||||||||||||||||||||||||

INGREDIENTS:

Any jar with a wide mouth opening
Fresh lavender, enough to loosely fill a jar
Honey (clover or wildflower), enough to completely fill a jar

DIRECTIONS:

- Fill your jar with fresh lavender (or fill it ¼ full if using dried lavender).
- Fill the jar right up to the top with clover or wildflower honey.
- Stir well.
- Cap the jar and put the preparation on a small plate, as it might get messy.
- Label the lid, not the jar, as honey might drip over and erase your label. (Your label should say whether you put in fresh or dried flowers, what kind of honey you used, and the date.)
- Let this blend sit for at least a month to be fully medicinal, though it will be delicious in just a day! If you can't resist having some before it's fully infused, stir in more honey to fill the jar back to the top after you sample it.

LAVENDER-COCONUT COOKIES

||||||||||||||||||||||||||||||||||||||||||||||||||||||||||||||||||

INGREDIENTS:

½ cup unsalted butter, softened, plus more for pan

½ cup coconut oil

1¼ cups coconut sugar (or less, to taste)

2 large free-range eggs

1 teaspoon vanilla extract

½ teaspoon almond extract

2¼ cups all-purpose flour (or Bob's Red Mill gluten-free baking flour)

4 teaspoons dried lavender flowers

1 teaspoon organic baking powder

½ teaspoon sea salt

DIRECTIONS:

○ Preheat oven to 375 degrees Fahrenheit.

○ In a bowl, cream butter, coconut oil, and coconut sugar until light and
fluffy. Add eggs, one at a time, beating well after each addition. Beat
in extracts. In a separate bowl, whisk flour, lavender, baking powder, and
salt; gradually beat into creamed mixture.

○ Drop by rounded teaspoonfuls 2 inches apart onto baking sheets
lightly coated with butter (or coconut oil).

○ Bake until golden brown, 8–10 minutes.

○ Cool for 2 minutes before moving to wire racks. Store in an
airtight container.

Lavender in Magic and Ritual

Freshly dried lavender retains the lovely fragrance of the fresh plant and can be used to bring sweetness to an outdoor area, or into your room or house at any time. It is a great herb to burn if you or anyone in your home have been having arguments. Lavender will help "clear the air" of the bad feeling that can remain after angry words have been spoken or yelled, or angry tears have been spilled. But nothing has to be wrong! Burn lavender to invite in the energy of play and delight. Another option is to put a couple handfuls of fragrant, dried lavender into a soup pot on the stove. Cover the herbs with freshly boiled water and leave the lid off to allow the lavender steam to sweeten the atmosphere. It's also a great way to help disinfect an area of airborne germs!

BURNING LAVENDER
DO THIS ONLY WITH AN ADULT PRESENT!

PLACE DRIED LAVENDER FLOWERS IN A FIRE-PROOF DISH, SUCH as an abalone shell, and use a lighter or match to light the flowers until the sweet-smelling smoke rises. Waft the smoke around an area or toward yourself with your hands or a feather. Enjoy!

A LAVENDER
BIRTHDAY PARTY RITUAL

PUT A FRESH BATCH OF COLD LAVENDER TEA INTO A SPRAY bottle. You and your friends gather in a circle with the one whose birthday is being celebrated in the center.

Have someone spray the person whose birthday it is with one small spritz of lavender tea, while everyone else calls out sweet birthday wishes for good things to come to them in the coming year. Then the birthday kid can spray all their friends as a way of saying "thank you," and all the partygoers get some sweetness, too! And while everyone is laughing, you can all have your birthday cake! Instant manifestation, with more sweet things to come!

You can also make an herbal bundle with lavender stalks, which then becomes a lavender magic wand!

LAVENDER MAGIC WAND

|||||||||||||||||||||||||||||||||||||||||||||||||||||||||||||||||||||||

YOU'LL NEED:

10 or more dried lavender stalks, in flower

Thin, natural fiber rope or thread

To make your own lavender wand, you will need to buy the lavender from an herb shop or garden market that sells lavender flowers that are still on the stalks, or you can grow the plants in your garden. If you are growing your own lavender, harvest the stalks when they are in flower in the summer, or anytime from late spring to early fall, depending on where you live. Hang them upside down out of direct sunlight until they are dry. Then, put your stalks together in a bundle with all the flowering tops facing the same way. Tie your thread in a tight knot about an inch from the bottom of the stalks and wrap the thread around and around the stalks on a diagonal all the way up to about an inch from the top, then diagonally criss-cross the thread back down to the starting knot. Secure the bundle with a few good knots, snip off any loose threads, and you have a lavender magic wand!

You can make this as described, and you can also combine it with Artemisia/mugwort stalks to make it even more magical—perfect for your meditations and magical workings!

LAVENDER SLEEP (AND/OR DREAM) PILLOW

Lavender is famous for helping us relax and sleep better. It is super-soothing on its own, but it can also be combined with other herbs to increase its healing power.

YOU'LL NEED:

Cotton, felt, or silk fabric scraps
(something that lets the scent come through)
Dried lavender flowers

Try adding any of the following with the lavender to address specific needs (optional): add an equal amount of dried catnip to make it even more helpful for sleeping; roses because they make your heart happy and smell good; and/or grandmother cedar (*Thuja occidentalis*) if you often have nightmares and feel afraid to go to sleep. Adjust amounts until you love how it smells.

You can make your pillow any shape and size you like!

Cut two pieces of fabric and sew them together, leaving one seam, or a few inches of space, open to be able to stuff the herbs in. Remember: your herbs must be totally dry!

Turn the fabric inside out, fill it with your dried herbs, then sew the last seam closed. You can leave the pillow simple, or you may choose to decorate it with beads, sequins, tiny seashells or crystals, feathers, or whatever you like! You can sew or glue on your decorations, or use fabric paint.

The first dream pillow I ever made was with two pieces of thin felt, one white and one black, in the shape of a crescent moon. I sewed tiny plastic pearls on the outside to be the stars and slept with it until it fell apart.

White Pine

(*PINUS STROBUS*)
PEACE AND FRIENDSHIP MAGIC

. . . .

Also known as: northern white pine, eastern pine
Pine says: "Be a good friend to yourself and others."

Meet White Pine

I'm an evergreen tree
with teachings to share.
Please treat one another
with kindness and care.
I have needles, not leaves,
that make a fine tea
And I'll help you to breathe
and not feel stuffy.
Make pine needle syrup
with buckwheat honey,
I calm coughs and help when
your nose is runny.

Inhale the aroma
of my fragrant wood.
Rich in vitamin C
I'll help you feel good.
I lift up your spirits,
and that's just the start,
As you breathe deeply, I'll
bring peace to your heart.
I will help you befriend
yourself and others,
All beings on Earth are
sisters and brothers.

Herbal Healing

Pine is most famous for being a healing herbal medicine for our respiratory system, especially our lungs. I love drinking pine needle infusions anytime, but especially in the fall and winter. Just as walking in the pine woods helps you feel calmer and encourages you to naturally breathe more slowly and deeply, drinking pine needle infusion will bring those gifts indoors, into your kitchen! Pine needle infusion is high in vitamin C and strengthens your immune system. It also supports your kidneys, helps you have clearer skin, promotes flexible joints, and uplifts your spirits!

Working with White Pine

Baby pine trees, from several inches to several feet tall, with soft green needles, dot the woods where I live, and their stately parent and grandparent trees watch over them from heights of fifty to eighty feet, sometimes reaching even one hundred feet tall. Higher up on the ridge are shorter pitch pines with much thicker dark green needles.

The familiar evergreen pine tree, the white pine, is called the "Tree of Peace" by the Indigenous peoples of the northeastern United States who call themselves the Haudenosaunee (how-de-no-saw-nee), or the "People of the Long House." They were originally composed of five, then later six, Indigenous tribes/nations who share the Iroquoian language. They were known as the Iroquois Confederacy, or the League of Nations, and had a direct influence on the men who wrote the US Constitution.

Though white pine is only native to the northeastern United States, it is abundant in many parts of the world. And if you don't have this species near you, there will always be another species of the generous pine to work with.

Pines with very dense, hard needles tend to be too high in resinous oils to taste good, whereas those with soft needles, like white pine and others, are both tasty and perfect for herbal healing. Nibbling on any pine needle is safe (of course, you first need to make sure it's a pine tree!).

All pines have the sour tang of ascorbic acid, better known as vitamin C, but the denser needles will taste bad, even gross, like turpentine! Spiritually, the Tree of Peace offers us a powerful, protective, and uplifting presence.

Identifying White Pine (and other pines)

All pines have needles that come in packets attached to the twigs and branches. White pine has five needles per packet. The way I remember this is that there is one needle for each letter: W-H-I-T-E.

Also, if you look very closely in good light, or through a magnifying glass, you'll see that a fine white stripe runs down the length of every soft, flexible needle on the white pine tree! The white pine is one of the tallest trees, growing as much as two to three feet every year. It is also adaptable and has become widely naturalized, growing in parks, yards, meadows, other woodlands, and on the edges of forests.

Pine is a graceful tree and has smooth, grayish bark when young and thickly ridged, brown bark when mature. The plume-like bundles of flexible needles are two to five inches long. Pine has both male and female cones (the fruits that house the seeds) growing on the same tree. Female cones tend to be about four to seven inches long with a purple-green tinge ripening to light brown when they mature in the fall. The cones open in the second year to disperse their seeds. Male cones are a half inch long, yellowish, and grow in clusters.

The most telltale sign for identifying white and other pine trees is the familiar scent. And though other evergreens such as spruces, hemlocks, and balsam firs will also have a refreshing, piney fragrance, their needles will be attached to the trees *singly*, not in packets. These trees are also used in herbal medicine, and they have some similar benefits to pine. Other evergreens that should *not* be used internally, such as yew trees, don't have needles in packets, nor do they have the uplifting smell associated with pine and other aromatic evergreens.

Gathering White Pine

One of the best ways to gather white pine is to go outside after a storm. These trees are experts at letting go. They shed their branches during heavy weather of all types—rain, snow, or wind storms. If the branches are freshly dropped off the trees, they are perfectly good to use for healing and for magic and ritual!

Otherwise, I suggest starting with harvesting the packets of needles and the tiniest twigs that come with them. As always, you start with connecting with the tree, offering a give-away and asking permission. If and when you are told "yes," you can proceed to harvest.

Here's a technique that the plants appreciate very much:

Put your thumb and index finger around a twig, just below where you intend to pinch off your bundle of needles. Ask the tree to breathe down below your fingers and pull their main life force energy back inward while sharing their gifts with you in the part you are taking/being given.

When you feel or imagine the tree has responded, pinch off the needles and put them in your paper bag or basket. Use a basket that you don't mind getting pine sap on! Gathering pine can be a sticky business. You'll discover that the tree will more readily give itself to you when you take the time to ask in this way!

Remember, green witchery and plant magic is not only about getting what you want; it's about growing loving relationships with other living beings who want to help you. They respond well to appreciation and respect, just like you and I do.

Creativity in the Kitchen

PINE NEEDLE INFUSION

||||||||||||||||||||||||||||||||||||||||||||||||||||||||||||||||

Pine needle infusions are yummy and can be drunk whether you are sick or not.

INGREDIENTS:

2 cups or more fresh pine needles, cut up into approximately 1-inch pieces
(use 1 cup or more if your pine is dried)

*Scissors are the best tool for cutting up your pine needles, though you can make
a meditation out of ripping up small bundles of needles by hand!

Boiling water

DIRECTIONS:

○ Put the needles into a ½-gallon jar and cover them with boiling water.

○ Cap tightly, and let sit for at least 8 hours. I usually leave my pine needle
  infusion to steep for 24 hours. Pour the infusion through a strainer
  before drinking.

QUICK METHOD FOR MAKING PINE NEEDLE TEA

||||||||||||||||||||||||||||||||||||||||||||||||||||||||||||||||

Put your cut-up pine needles into a stainless steel or enamel pot. Cover the
needles with cold water, filling the pot. Bring the water up to a boil, then turn
off the flame. Cover the pot and let your infusion sit and steep the same way
as you would in the jar, but you can start drinking your tea in 30 minutes after
straining. It will get tastier and even more healing the longer it sits, but it will be
delightful and helpful made in this way, too.

TIP: Put a bit of olive oil on a rag or paper towel and wipe down your scissors, pot, or jar before washing them in soap and water. This will make getting the sticky sap off your tools much easier. It is also the best method I've found for cleaning your hands of pine sap . . . soap and water alone don't quite do the job!

WINTER COLD RELIEF REMEDY

This is a wonderful healing brew to drink when you have a cold. I like to make this blend at the Winter Solstice, too, as it looks like winter in your jar! Remember that herbs aren't just medicine for when you're sick—you can use them to build and maintain good health in the first place!

INGREDIENTS:

1 cup or more fresh pine needles, cut up into ½–1-inch pieces
(use ½ cup or more if your pine is dried)

¼–½ cup rose hips

¼–½ cup elder blossoms

Honey, to taste (optional)

DIRECTIONS:

- Blend all plant ingredients in a 1-quart jar.
- Pour boiling water over the herbs.
- Let them sit for one hour (or more).
- Pour off the herbs, and remember that when they are cool enough, squeeze them to get the last precious ounce or so of the herbal tea.
- Drink and enjoy. You can add honey to taste if you like.

PINE NEEDLE SYRUP

||||||||||||||||||||||||||||||||||||||||||||||||||||||||||||||||||||||

This recipe is great to make ahead of time and keep ready and waiting in the refrigerator if you come down with a cold, cough, or the flu, or to take by the spoonful to fortify your respiratory and immune systems during cold and flu season. Used that way, it is useful for preventing colds and flus.

Start with the pine needle infusion recipe on page 100. After the infusion has steeped for a minimum of 8 hours (up to 24 hours), pour off the liquid into an enamel or stainless steel saucepan.

Put the needles themselves into a square of cheesecloth and squeeze them to get every drop of liquid out. Whenever possible, compost the herbs.

Now, put the pot on the lowest possible flame and keep an eye on it, as you are looking to have the liquid turn to steam that rises from the top, but not bubble in the pot. This is called making a "decoction." If you start with a half gallon of infusion, you'll steam it down by half and end up with 1 quart. If you start with 1 quart, you'll steam it until it is down to 1 pint. Note that the more liquid you start with, the longer it takes.

When the volume is half the original amount, remove the decoction from the stove and add approximately 1 tablespoon of honey for each cup of decoction. You can absolutely add more if you like it sweeter. The honey also acts as a preservative and is helpful for easing a dry cough.

Voilà! You have made pine needle syrup! Stored in the fridge in a capped glass bottle, it will keep for 2–3 months!

PINE NEEDLE HONEY

||||||||||||||||||||||||||||||||||||||||||||||||||||||||||||||||

I LOVE pine needle honey, and it is super easy to make.

Cut or finely tear up pine needles and put them into a wide-mouth jar, filling the jar almost to the top. Cover with local wildflower honey, or buckwheat honey, or whatever kind you like the best, filling the jar all the way to the top.

Let your infused honey sit in the jar for *at least* a month atop a saucer. When you're ready to use it, put the bottle, still capped, into a hot water bath to warm it up until the honey flows like water. Pour it through a strainer and you'll have a divine infused honey to put in tea, on toast, into your pine needle syrup, or even to use for a wonderful facial mask!

Do NOT throw out or compost those needles yet! The next time you are making any kind of tea, put the sticky needles in there, too, and they will infuse your tea with the last of that delicious pine honey.

White Pine in Magic and Ritual

Pines are not only one of the oldest species of trees on the planet, but, like all evergreens, they remind us that there is something eternal that lives within us, and beyond our human lifetime. Something ever-green and growing. Pine loves to help you be flexible enough to let go of unwanted stuff that is weighing you down, anything you are carrying that may be keeping you from inner peace or from being a good friend to yourself. It can be an attitude, like thinking you aren't good enough and need to be perfect, or maybe a fear you have of saying what you really think or feel, or it could be something you feel mad or hurt about that you'd really like to get past.

SPIRITUAL BATHING RITUAL
WITH PINE WANDS

THIS RITUAL IS BEST DONE WITH YOUR FAMILY OR FRIENDS. IT will bring you closer together and help everyone who participates to feel peaceful inside, and that promotes good relationships. It can be done any-time, or you might do this ritual because it's needed, for example soon after blending two families together, or when someone you care about is feeling anxious for some reason and you want to help them.

Find a beautiful pine branch, from 1–3 feet long, still green, that has fallen from the tree, to be your magic pine wand.

If a freshly fallen branch is not available, you can use a pair of pruning clippers to cut a thin branch off the tree. You may need an adult to help you. If you need to cut it, it will be best to clip a thin branch that is growing out of another *branch*, rather than growing directly from the tree trunk. Cut it as closely and cleanly as you can, then, after you cut it, be sure to put your fingertips on the cut place on the tree and send your love and gratitude to the tree for their gift.

You'll also need to gather enough pine needles to make a big pot of pine needle tea. Feel free to put other herbs in there, too—perhaps some roses or lavender. After it's come to a boil, turn off the heat and let it steep, with the cover off, leaving it long enough to cool down completely.

While it is steeping and cooling, you can dance to loosen up! Or take a walk. Or write or draw. Or meditate. When it's time, decant the herbs, pouring off the liquid and giving the herbs to the earth. Then get into pairs. Each person will take a turn at dipping the pine wand into the tea. Holding onto the wand firmly, shake the tea onto your friend. Then it's their turn to "bathe" you with the magic brew.

Next, one of you will tap the branch on the ground nine times while you both imagine everything you released with love, trust, and the help of the Tree of Peace, being absorbed for you by the Earth. Now it is immediately transforming into fertile compost to grow your inner peace and friendship, to extend to yourself and others.

Finally, go somewhere you can give the pine wands back to the Earth, and toss them as far away as you can.

Say, "Blessed be," and walk away. Don't look back. Trust the magic will unfold! It is a fun, meaningful ritual and truly helps, as you'll see!

Dandelion

(*TARAXACUM OFFICINALE*)
RESILIENCE AND LIGHT-UP-THE-DARKNESS MAGIC

. . . .

Also known as: lion's tooth, pis-en-lis, clock flower, Irish daisy
Dandelion says: "Root in the Earth, shine like the Sun."

Meet Dandelion

I am so common
You might not notice me
Nor how special I am
As you will soon see
My yellow flowers
Brighten up any lawn
Though often cursed as weeds
I do you no wrong
I support your lymph
And strengthen your liver
I nourish your kidneys
I'm a great giver

I help clear your skin
And tone your digestion
Please do get to know me
That's my suggestion
My flowers will ease pain
When you feel stuck and mired
My mineral-rich leaves
Help when you're tired
I'm a complex plant
Deep, dark, and yet sunny
Brown roots in the soil
I'm golden like honey.

Herbal Healing

All parts of dandelions support the immune system by helping lymph fluid flow freely. The roots are best known for helping the liver, while the leaves are known for overall nourishment and support of the kidneys. The flowers are delicious to eat and can be turned into oils and ointments. Flowers are also said to help ease emotional pain that is stuck in the body.

Working with Dandelion

Everyone knows dandelions, or at least they think they do! There is so much here to love! Dandelions are widespread around the world, and through the spring, summer, and fall they offer us gifts from their roots, leaves, flowers, and seeds. During the winter months, dandelions store sugars, starches, and everything they need to stay alive and nourished until the warming sun and thawing ground invite them to grow upward toward the surface world again, with roots that are a bit thicker and juicier than the year before. The long roots of dandelions are called "tap roots," and they excel at revitalizing soil. They bring minerals up from depths below the surface and make them available to all the plants growing there.

Did you know that plants not only heal people and other-than-human animals, but also the land itself? Weeds like dandelions are called "bioaccumulators"—they accumulate nutrients by pulling them up into themselves through their long roots. When the plants die back to the earth and decompose, those minerals are distributed throughout the upper layers of soil to nourish new dandelions and other plants, too.

Identifying Dandelions

Of course, you can't identify dandelions when they are under the ground, but you can memorize where you last saw them and start to watch for them to rise out of the earth again in the spring. An everyday sort of miracle when you really think about it! They grow out of the top of the root (a.k.a. the crown) and sprout cotyledons (kah-ta-lee-dens), the first tender leaves of any plant to emerge above the soil. Dandelions are yellow-green, smooth, and circular to oval. These will grow into light to dark green leaves that may have some hairs, but are generally smooth. They have a strong midrib that is often, but not always, red, and mostly toothed leaf "margins" (the outer edges of the leaves), though the size of the "teeth" can vary, with some leaves even having nearly smooth margins. If you see a fine line of hairs along the midrib on the underside of the leaf, you are seeing chicory, not dandelion. Looking out for that line of hair is a fun exercise, and it's a great way to make sure you have found dandelion, not chicory. When these two plants are in flower, it is super easy to tell them apart because chicory has blue flowers, but in their pre-flowering stage, they look nearly identical (at least, until you look closely, as green witch herbalists like to do!).

Dandelion plants grow in rosettes, each leaf growing out from the center to form an ever-expanding circle of layers of leaves. At some point, a slightly hairy but mostly smooth, hollow stalk grows up right out of the center of the rosette. This is the flower stalk. It tastes bitter and has some white juice in it. That juice is naturally occurring latex. The funny thing is, bitter tastes, in general, help to balance the sugar in our blood! I nibble these flower stalks in the spring to do exactly that! The root and leaves contain this latex, too. The flowers start as tightly curled up buds that unfurl into the familiar bright, sunny flower. These flowers open each day and close at night, giving the plant the nickname of "clock flower." The flowers also close if rain is coming. The secret about dandelion blossoms is that each "petal" is actually a complete flower! Ultimately, the flower will close up again before it goes to seed, then open to reveal that a beautiful, silvery-white ball of seeds has been formed. The seeds will be spread by the wind on their parachute-like sails.

It's said that symbolically the flowers are the Sun, the seed head is the Moon, and the seeds are the stars!

In the fall, at the tail end of the growing season, the stalk that the seed head is atop can shoot up as much as another inch overnight. That makes it easier for the seeds to be picked up and spread by the wind. This is nature's genius at work!

Gathering Dandelions

In the early spring, dandelion flowers are a prime food source for bees and other pollinators. It is unfortunate that some people still pull, or worse yet, poison them to have "perfect" lawns! What could be more beautiful than a field of golden wildflowers abuzz with visiting bees, butterflies, moths, and more?

As with any plant, you need to learn *when* to harvest the part you want. So, for example, the best dandelion leaves to harvest for food and medicine are in the spring and fall, before and after the flowers. When you harvest leaves from the rosette, gather from the innermost base of each leaf. Dandelions tend to grow in abundance, so you can usually harvest freely.

The flowers themselves begin in early spring and often continue for many months! You can pinch just the flower tops off or gather the whole stalk, depending on what you're going to do with them (read on for the possibilities!). Briefly touch a fingertip to the opening you've left, whether atop the stalk or at the rosette, to "seal" it energetically.

The roots can be dug in the spring or the fall. I most often dig autumn dandelion roots because I want to get them when they are pulling their nutrients back into themselves for the winter. This way, they will nourish *me* through the winter. The roots can go down three feet, but six to twelve inches is more the average. You will want to use a hand trowel and a digging fork as you move around the root in a circle, loosening up the soil and digging down and down, starting about six inches or so out from the center of the plant to unearth the entire root. I do recommend washing roots before making anything with them. You can use a little scrub brush, too, if needed.

Gathering leaves, flower stalks, and flowers is easy and fun! Digging roots takes more work and determination but feels very rewarding when you've done it, especially when you are patient and dig until you get the entire root! Now let's explore some of the gifts dandelions are best known for and the various ways you can take this wonderful plant into yourself.

Creativity in the Kitchen

The leaves can be eaten raw in salads, and they provide a remarkable array of vitamins and minerals such as vitamin C, beta-carotene (vitamin A), calcium, potassium, and iron. They can also be cooked in any dishes that call for cooked greens like spinach or kale. Leaves keep well in the refrigerator, much like store-bought greens, except that since they are wild, they're a bit more robust and will last longer! You can buy some cultivated dandelion leaves in the store and compare. The cultivated ones may look more "perfect," but the wild ones will have more flavor and be richer in vitamins and minerals, as well as the other nutrients they contain. Dandelion leaves can also be dried for tea and to be used in cooking.

The flowering stalks can be cut up and added to salads and cooking greens, or eaten as is. They can also be harvested to get their latex, which when dabbed directly on warts and skin tags consistently will dissolve them over time. Plant magic!

DANDELION LEAF AND FLOWER SALAD

||||||||||||||||||||||||||||||||||||||||||||||||||||||||||||||||||||||||||

INGREDIENTS:

1 cup or more fresh dandelion leaves

1 cup fresh dandelion flowers

Other greens (optional)

DIRECTIONS:

- Make a salad using either all dandelion leaves or whatever others you like, such as red leaf lettuce, Boston lettuce, spinach, mesclun, and/or arugula. Put in at least 1 cup, or up to an equal amount, of dandelion leaves. Shred a cup of the blossoms by pulling the flower rays (petals) out from the center of the flower head and add those in. When you've tossed the salad, add some whole flowers to the top for edible beauty. Serve with whatever dressing you like, although I recommend olive oil and balsamic vinegar, or a mustard vinaigrette.

DANDELION PESTO

INGREDIENTS:

¼ cup walnuts, pumpkin seeds, or pine nuts

5 cloves garlic (or to taste)

1 cup fresh dandelion leaves

1 cup fresh basil leaves

¾ cup olive oil

Sea salt, to taste

DIRECTIONS:

- You can use the traditional mortar and pestle method and blend the ingredients together coarsely, or use a food processor and make a smooth pesto. Start with the nuts or seeds, then add the garlic, then your greens, then your olive oil, and finally, salt to taste. Serve this over pasta, vegetables, or on avocado toast—yum!
- Refrigerate any leftovers.

DANDELION ROOT SWEET TONIC SYRUP

||||||||||||||||||||||||||||||||||||||||||||||||||||||||||||||||

When taken daily by teaspoon, this tonic is good for your digestion, provides iron and energy, and is generally supportive for your immune system.

INGREDIENTS:

¾ cup dried dandelion roots

½ cup honey

2 tablespoons blackstrap molasses

DIRECTIONS:

○ Pour boiling water over the dandelion roots in a 1-quart jar and let steep overnight.

○ Pour off the infusion through a strainer into an open saucepan.

○ Put the roots into a piece of cheesecloth and twist the cloth to squeeze out every drop of liquid you can from the roots.

○ Turn the stove to the lowest possible setting and dip a utensil into the liquid to mark the level.

○ When the steam begins to rise, check the level as often as you like as the liquid in the pot is slowly reduced by half.

○ Once you have about 1 pint, take the pot off the heat and stir in the honey and the molasses.

○ Pour into your jar and label its contents.

○ Store it in the refrigerator.

*Note: It will keep for at least a month, but if you take it daily it won't last that long!

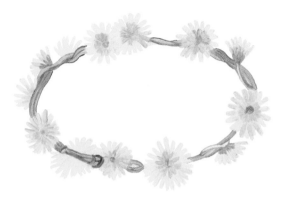

Dandelion in Magic and Ritual

Dandelion flowers make great crowns (or necklaces) for spring and early summer rituals. They won't last long, but you will feel wild, witchy, and wonderful when you wear them atop your head or around your neck at a magical gathering!

HOW TO WEAVE THEM, THE SUPER SIMPLE WAY: Gather a bunch of dandelions. Cut the stalks down to about 3 inches in length. Use a fork tine, or any similar pointy tool, to poke a hole in the middle of a stalk. Thread the next dandelion through that hole, poke a hole in the middle of that stem, and continue until you have a long enough weave of dandelions to wear atop your head or around your neck. Tie the flowers together in several places, as needed, with thread or thin yarn; perhaps choose a color you like to go with the yellow and green. Trim any stalk ends that are sticking out too far. Everyone looks good in flowers!

HOW TO WEAVE THEM, MORE INTRICATELY: If you want a thick wreath or crown of dandelion flowers, try the following method.

Keep the stalks long when you gather your dandelion flowers. Take 6 long-stemmed dandelions, divide them into three parts, and start to braid them together like hair. Each time you wrap the stems over, add two more dandelions. Wrap the other side over the newly added dandelions and so on. When you flip the crown over, the back will look like a beautiful braid! When it is the size you want for your wreath or crown, there will be loose stems left over at the end. Now pull the ends together and wrap the loose ends into the rest of the braid, securing them between the dandelion flowers. Continue wrapping the loose ends into the flower heads until they are all secured. You can wear these for any occasion! And you might want to wear them while you do the next ritual!

DANDELION SEED WISHES

THIS IS A MAGICAL RITUAL THAT ALMOST EVERYONE KNOWS, but it is timeless! Gather a stalk with a beautiful round seed head on top to make a special wish. When you are ready to make the wish, blow on the Moon-shaped seed head and send those star seeds that represent your wish out to the "four winds." Remember to put a give-away gift down for the dandelion plant to say "thank you" for the star seeds and for helping you state your wish to the universe! The dandelion may thank you, too, because you are also planting new dandelions for next spring!

Plantain

(*PLANTAGO MAJOR* AND *P. LANCEOLATA*)
SIMPLE FUN MAGIC

· ·

Also known as: ribwort, broadleaf, band-aid, white man's foot
Plantain says: "Keep it simple. Keep it fun."

Meet Plantain

I'm a green band-aid
And grow in big patches.
I clean out your cuts
And patch up your scratches.
If you are bleeding
Or get an infection,
I know what to do
To give you protection.
I'm also tasty
And full of nourishment.

I keep it simple
No need to flourish it.
I grow in your lawns,
And do so many things.
I like to have fun,
Use my seed stalks as slings!
Kids are my closest friends,
I tell you it's true.
You are my favorites
I hope you'll love me, too.

Herbal Healing

Plantain is such a humble weed, yet is highly valued just about everywhere in the world where people have herbal medicine traditions. I take a plantain salve with me wherever I go to help with bumps, bruises, paper cuts, drawing out splinters, and especially to relieve itching from bug bites.

Plantain excels at drawing out foreign objects like splinters, stingers, or slivers of glass and helps prevent infections. Plantain brings down swelling, quickly relieves pain and itching, slows down and stops bleeding, helps clean out wounds before and after soap and water can be applied, and this simple weed has proven effective at localizing poisons so they don't spread. It is a natural antiseptic—"anti-sepsis" means "against infection." Always apply plantain externally after a tick has been removed! This will reduce local irritation and can help prevent the spread of harmful bacteria whether you've been prescribed antibiotics or not.

The leaves, eaten fresh in salads, cooked into sautés, or dried and made into tea, bring healing to the belly and lungs and provide an abundance of iron, calcium, vitamins A and C, and chlorophyll, the substance that makes plants green. Chlorophyll is almost identical to the iron in our blood, and it helps keeps our blood healthy and red as it flows through our arteries to deliver nourishment all around our bodies.

Plantain also strengthens our veins, the thinner pathways the blood travels through to come back to our heart and lungs to receive fresh oxygen when we inhale. Then the whole process starts all over again. Did you know that your blood makes a complete round trip of your body in about one minute, and it does this every minute of every day? Aren't we amazing?

Working with Plantain

I've often said that if I could only have one plant, I would choose plantain!

That's a big thing for a green witch to say, what with so many plants to choose from, but here's why—little plantain grows almost everywhere, does so many different things to heal our bodies, and does no harm! From salad greens, to cough medicine, to "spit poultices" that stop bleeding, itching, and swelling, plantain does it all!

Identifying Plantain

Plantain is a weed/wild plant that pops up anywhere and everywhere. You can find plantain in the cracks in the sidewalks, in meadows and fields, and, perhaps most abundantly, in people's lawns!

Sometimes people get confused and think we are talking about the delicious tropical fruit that is also called plantain, or *plátano* in Spanish. But that plant is a fruiting tree, closely related to bananas. This is why green witch herbalists learn the botanical/Latin names of plants. Nicknames or common names overlap, so the same name will often be used for different plants.

The plantain I'm talking about is a plant that grows close to the ground, and like our friend dandelion, the leaves open out from the center in a rosette. But plantain's leaves have a quality that is fairly rare and can help you in your identification skills. The veins on each leaf run parallel to one another, from the bottom where it grows out of the rosette, up to the leaf tip. The more common pattern is for there to be one central vein, or midrib, such as we see in a dandelion leaf, with veins branching out to the leaf's margins from there.

Another helpful identification tip is to count the veins. You'll see there are five, seven, or nine of them. The easiest way to do this is to turn the leaf over because the veins are more prominent on the underside of the leaf. You can rub your finger over them and feel how they stand out from the leaf.

Plantain is a fiber-rich plant, and you can even separate those stringy veins from the leaves and use them as trailside dental floss! (They'll break easier than "real" floss but will definitely work in a pinch!) The size of plantain varies a lot. In lawns where they are mowed over and over again, the plants will be tiny, just a few inches all the way around. But in a place where they are allowed to grow, the leaves can be quite large, each one being six to eight inches from bottom to tip, so the whole plant might take up one foot of space or more. It is highly unusual to see just one plantain plant, though it can happen. Typically, you'll see a lot of them growing near one another. Late in the summer, into fall, the plant will send up a central flower/seed stalk. The flowers are so tiny you really have to look closely to see them. Their color ranges from white to light pink. They grow on the top of a spike, and later, the flowers are followed by small, brown seeds that are either at the top or grow up and down the central stalk, depending on which species of plantain you are looking at.

Gathering Plantain

I love to harvest this abundant plant, especially the leaves, and one day a plantain plant "told" me a special way to do so, and I want to share it with you.

Once you've offered your give-away and asked for and received permission to harvest, lightly put the thumb and index finger of one hand on the plant, right in the very center of the rosette, as if to hold the plant in place. With your other hand, use a fingernail like a knife and take the leaf off with a crescent moon–shaped movement, as if you are drawing the letter C. I use my thumbnail. With some practice it will become easy and natural.

Plantain leaves can be gathered in spring, summer, and fall. I usually do my best to gather them when they are not in seed, so the leaves will have more of their energy (i.e., vitamins and minerals). The seeds are gathered in late summer and autumn, whenever they are ripe. You know the seeds are ripe when you take a few off the stalk and taste them, or try to squish them in your fingertips. If they are still soft and mushy, no matter if they are white or brown, they're not ready. When they're ready to harvest, they'll be brown and a little chewy, and they'll have a similar texture to sunflower seeds (minus their shells).

I gather whole seedstalks and store them in a paper bag. You can also strip off the seeds and store those in a glass jar.

Creativity in the Kitchen

Fresh plantain leaves are delicious in a salad! You can use the broad leaf or the narrow leaf varieties, whichever you have around you. The younger, smaller leaves are tender and have a rather nutty taste. Tear or cut them up into small pieces and add the leaves freely to salads, or include them in your sandwiches. The leaves can also be sautéed with other vegetables! There is no better nourishment for us than adding some wild greens to our meals!

There are a number of great things you'll want to know how to make with plantain leaves for topical use on your skin. The first is a "spit poultice."

SPIT POULTICE

A spit poultice is the most direct and effective way to apply this plant for immediate healing. It comes in handy whenever you are outside playing and get hurt, whether you've fallen and gotten banged up, or you've scraped your knees and are bleeding, it's plantain to the rescue! A plantain spit poultice is also the perfect medicine if you get stung by a mosquito, bee, or wasp, or even for a spider bite.

DIRECTIONS:

○ Gather one or more leaves, depending on how big an area you need to cover. Take them from plantain plants that are clean. You can wipe off the leaves you've gathered with your fingers to make sure there is no loose dirt on them, then chew them just enough to break up the leaf and make it juicy. If you wish, you can give the leaves a quick cold water rinse before chewing them.

○ Put that green mash on your skin if you've been hurt or stung. You've made a living green band-aid! It will stick to your skin for a while, or you can hold it there. Sometimes, if needed, you can apply an actual band-aid, or a strip of cloth that you pin closed over the leaf, to hold it in place.

○ Plantain is anti-infective, and there are enzymes in your saliva that mix with properties in the plant to make it even more anti-infective than it is already!

PLANTAIN POULTICE

||||||||||||||||||||||||||||||||||||||||||||||||||||||||||||||||||||||||

If you prefer, you can make a traditional, non-spit poultice.

Bruise fresh or dry leaves with whatever is handy, such as a rock outside or a mortar and pestle inside. Pour just enough boiled water to cover, and after they've steeped for 5–10 minutes, remove them from the water using whatever tool is handy and apply them when they've cooled down, which generally takes about 10–15 seconds.

Preparing a plantain-infused oil and/or a salve is a wise thing to do. It is such a handy item to have in your first aid kit at home and to take with you. When you don't have access to fresh leaves, you'll be able to rely on your oil or salve.

You'll need to wilt the leaves a bit before you make the oil, which means drying them, but not as fully as you do for tea.

DRYING OR WILTING PLANTAIN LEAVES

||||||||||||||||||||||||||||||||||||||||||||||||||||||||||||||||||||||||

After you've gathered your plantain leaves, which you want to do on a nice, dry day, spread them out on screens or wicker trays and baskets to dry.

Turn them over once or twice as they are drying. Or take a sewing needle and thread and pierce each plantain leaf's stalk a half inch to an inch down and pull the needle through all the leaves you've gathered, then spread them out so none are touching each other.

You can use push pins to secure each end of your plantain "clothesline" into a wall as your leaves are drying. Needless to say, they look beautiful hanging up this way! Make sure they are not in direct sunlight as that will bleach out their chlorophyll and make them less medicinal. You know they are dry when you bend the leaves and they crack. I store mine in paper bags labeled with the common name of the plant (Plantain), the botanical name, such as *Plantago lanceolata*, and the month I gathered them. Add the place, too, if you like.

For the oil or ointment, you don't need to fully dry them, nor will you be storing them for later use. You simply need to give some of the moisture in the plant a chance to evaporate before infusing the leaves in oil. Water and oil do not mix well, and combining them can lead to mold.

So you wilt them, which means to partially dry them for 24–48 hours.

PLANTAIN-INFUSED OIL

||||||||||||||||||||||||||||||||||||||||||||||||||||||||||||

- Tear or cut up your partially dried leaves and put them into a totally dry glass jar with a fairly wide opening and a tight-fitting lid (plastic or metal).
- When the jar is almost full, poke through the leaves to the bottom of your jar in a few places.
- Slowly fill the jar to the tippy-top with olive oil, making sure to keep poking to create space so all the leaves get thoroughly soaked. Make sure that no leaves are sticking up out of the oil, or they could mold. (If this happens, and if the mold is only there on top, carefully spoon that part out, wipe the inner rim of the jar out with a clean, dry rag or paper towel, and add fresh olive oil to refill.)
- Cap your jar and set it on top of a plate or in a bowl because oil will usually seep out from under the lid and drip over the sides of the jar as natural gases are released from the leaves. I suggest labeling your plantain oil on the lid rather than on the side of the jar for that reason.
- It is a good idea to store this oil in a cool, dry place and check on it every few days to make sure no leaves are sticking up. If they are, just push them back down or take them out. You can also poke around again to release gas bubbles from the plant, then add more oil if needed to bring the level back to the top.
- Decant your oil after 2–4 weeks.
- Pour off the oil into a clean, dry jar.
- Squeeze the leaves to get the oil from them, too.
- Cap and label your jar of plantain oil. It's ready to use now!

TIP: There is one more step that I recommend. By the next day you will see that there is a layer of a different color on the very bottom of your jar. This is a layer of water. When you see this layer, slowly pour the oil into another clean, dry jar, and just leave the last little bit, which still has the water layer, behind. You can use that oil, but use it up quickly rather than storing it because it won't stay fresh as long. By removing it, your newly labeled bottle of oil will stay fresh much longer.

PLANTAIN OINTMENT
|||||||||||||||||||||||||||||||||||||||||||||||||||||||||||||||

Plantain oil and ointment are also helpful for rashes,
dry skin, and even pimples.

INGREDIENTS:
2 ounces plantain-infused oil
1 teaspoon grated beeswax

DIRECTIONS:
- Pour your plantain-infused oil into a saucepan set to the lowest heat.
- Add 1 teaspoon of grated beeswax, stirring quickly until the beeswax is completely melted.
- Pour the mixture back into the jar. Cap it.
- You can watch your oil turn to ointment from the bottom up. It takes about 10 minutes to become solid and ready for use.
- Label your jar as usual.

TIP: One advantage of ointment is it is less messy to take with you than a bottle of oil. Use it exactly the same way.

ROASTED PLANTAIN SNACK

||||||||||||||||||||||||||||||||||||||||||||||||||||||||||||||

INGREDIENTS:

¼ cup plantain seeds

½ cup hemp seeds

½ cup pumpkin seeds

¾ cup shelled sunflower seeds

Sea salt, to taste

Dried thyme or marjoram, crumbled, to taste (optional)

Garlic powder, to taste (optional)

Olive oil

DIRECTIONS:

○ Preheat oven to 250 degrees Fahrenheit.

○ Put the seeds, sea salt, and herbs and garlic (if using) into a bowl.

○ Drizzle with olive oil and stir well to make sure the seeds are coated. Add more if needed.

○ Spread out the seed mixture onto unbleached parchment paper and bake for 10–15 minutes.

○ Let cool.

○ Enjoy sprinkled on salads, over cooked vegetables, or as a tasty snack.

Plantain in Magic and Ritual

Plantain is so abundant and accessible that it can be easy to underestimate. Most of us have been taught that the harder something is to come by, the more we should value it. But that is not the way of nature. As green witches know, Earth is generous with her blessings, bringing the plants we most need close to us, and you can't get much closer than plantain, who is most often right underfoot!

Plantain has so much magic to share, including enhancing the virtues of other plants.

Way back in the tenth century, plantain was one of the Nine Sacred Herbs, or Nine Herbs Charm, a protective blend that was sacred to the Anglo-Saxons and invoked the Norse god Odin. Plantain is believed to be the herb referred to as "waybread," and another of our plant friends, mugwort, is also one of those nine sacred herbs!

The physical and spiritual attributes of our plant allies always mirror each other. Plantain is physically *and* magically protective. It can also help you *draw in* the kinds of energy and experiences that you are looking to bring into your life.

Never ask the plants to help you *make* someone else do something. That is unwise. It goes against the ethics of a real green witch. On top of that, *it will always backfire*, immediately or after a while.

CRAFTING A SPELL WITH PLANTAIN

HARVEST ENOUGH LEAVES TO PLACE THEM IN A ROSETTE shape, mirroring the way the plant grows. Use at least four leaves, one for east, south, west, and north, and position them as such.

Glue them into a fresh page in your green witch book.

To do an invoking spell, imagine that each leaf is an arrow pointing inward.

Put something that represents YOU right in the center, nestled into the safety and protection of lovely plantain. This could be a photo, a drawing, your name, or something else that symbolizes you.

(There is plenty of room for your individual creativity here, so I'm giving you a few ideas, and you and your friends can take it from there!)

Paint, draw, or write words under or over each leaf that say what you want to attract, such as fun, true friends, good health, confidence, creativity, to feel understood, to feel safe, etc.

Place your hands on the rosette and recite this spell rhyme, or one you create:

Plantain, help me feel happy and free.
Plantain, I know this is meant to be.
Thank you for sending these blessings to me!
"Blessed Be and May the Greatest Good of All Be Served."

(I use this last line as a closing incantation for any spell I do.)

Say the spell with your whole heart, repeating that invocation nine times on the night of the full moon, or nine times three nights in a row. If you choose to do the spell over three nights, begin the night before the full moon, the night of, and the night following.

Then, open to receive the magical blessings as they come your way!

Conclusion

. . . .

Connecting with Plant Magic
to Transform Our Lives and Our World

WE'VE EXPLORED HOW PLANTS AND RITUALS CAN HELP YOU transform your health and your life, how they can help you discover who you truly are. Plants and magical rituals help you become confident in being your unique self, and in knowing you are a beautiful, loved, and loving part of nature.

But what about the world we live in together? It surely needs transforming. Don't we want to live in a world that is peaceful and just, a world where everyone has enough to eat and drink and can live healthy lives? Though it may seem like an impossible dream, it can happen, with your help.

Everything that becomes manifest in the world begins in *someone's* imagination. Every new invention, every city, every new technological advance, every food recipe, anything that exists originates in the creative cauldron of our imaginations.

A possibility for change starts as a notion, floating around in the ether, just waiting for someone to grasp it and form it into an idea in their mind. And the world doesn't transform all at once. We begin to change it by changing something in our own corner of the world.

Kids, guided by adults, working in partnership with each other, the plants, and nature can accomplish so much!

It could be something like, "Some of our neighbors don't have enough food to eat," or even simply, "People need to go outside more! Let's start an organic garden for our block or town or apartment building residents to share."

Or:

"Let's meet with our mayor and the town officials to show them that they can use certain mushrooms to heal the soil of the contaminants left behind by a polluting industry."

Or:

"Let's find out which plants help clean water, get our whole school to plant them along this riverbank, and bring it back to health!"

All these examples are real ideas that were dreamed up and then happened! They then inspired new healing projects. Plants are such skillful and generous healers. When we connect with them, respecting the more-than-human world of nature, we can accomplish what we cannot without them. Please realize that plants or mushrooms that are cleaning water or land absorb and break down contaminants in their own bodies. They are performing a service for us. We can and must express our gratitude for their work on our behalf, but please remember that they would no longer be safe to eat or make medicine with. Did you know that sunflowers can absorb radioactivity from water and soil, neutralizing it with their own bodies? We have so much more to learn about the healing gifts of the plants.

Meanwhile, experience teaches that if we can imagine it, we can help bring it into being with our actions, including our magical ones that help us envision what to do next.

Young green witches are definitely going to be the change-makers if you are not already!

Recognizing your relationship within the web of life changes how you see everything. Our elders, the plants, guide us into our own wisdom because they are wise in the ways of kinship and community. They are generous and teach us to be generous, too. They know how to live together and support one another.

They help you gain the confidence you need to grow into adults who will raise your voices in full support of healing the world we love.

Coming into a relationship with plants deepens all your relationships.

We are truly all in this together.

Listening to the plants makes us wiser.

And coming together in community helps us to be stronger and braver.

If we can't imagine that what we're hoping for is possible, it cannot materialize in the day-to-day world. But every uplifting transformation begins with a desire to bring about change. Let's dream together, with each other and the plants, and we will bring our dreams into being.

Here is a traditional closing blessing green witches say to one another three times at the end of our ritual gatherings:

Merry meet,
Merry part, and
Merry meet again.

Merry meet,
Merry part, and
Merry meet again.

Merry meet,
Merry part, and
Merry meet again.

Blessed be.

About the Author
and Illustrator

. . . .

ROBIN ROSE BENNETT has been writing, teaching, and practicing green witchery locally and internationally for over thirty years. Once dubbed "The Green Witch of New York," she now lives in New Jersey with her extensive herbal gardens where she enjoys inspiring and empowering a new generation of green witches.

RACHEL GRANT is an artist, designer, and illustrator based in North Staffordshire, UK. Her hand painted, textural artwork is often inspired by slow, simple living and she aims to capture moments of calm in everything she creates. When she's not at her desk painting, she enjoys gardening, pottery, knitting, and baking fresh bread.